# THE CHRISTIAN MEANING OF
## THE OLD TESTAMENT

# THE
# CHRISTIAN MEANING
# OF
# THE OLD TESTAMENT

NORBERT LOHFINK, S.J.

Translated by R. A. Wilson

THE BRUCE PUBLISHING COMPANY / MILWAUKEE

*221.1*
*LOC*

NIHIL OBSTAT:
RICHARD J. SKLBA, S.S.L., S.T.D.
Censor librorum

IMPRIMATUR:
✠ WILLIAM E. COUSINS
Archbishop of Milwaukee
April 18, 1968

This is a translation of Das Siegeslied am Schilfmeer, published in German by Verlag Josef Knecht, 1965.

*221.1*

Library of Congress Catalog Card Number: 68-28444
COPYRIGHT © 1968 THE BRUCE PUBLISHING COMPANY
MADE IN THE UNITED STATES OF AMERICA

# PREFACE TO THE AMERICAN EDITION

Norbert Lohfink's *Das Siegeslied am Schilfmeer* (*The Victory Song at the Sea of Reeds*) was published in German in 1965. The title of the English translation, which describes the nature of the work far more clearly than the German title, is inspired by the subtitle of the German version, "Christliche Auseinandersetzungen mit dem Alten Testament" (literally, "Christian Encounters with the Old Testament"). For the work is, in essence, a Christian conversation with the Old Testament, an attempt by a man of Christian faith to grasp the enduring significance of the sacred writings of the Hebrews which form an integral part of the Scriptures of the Christian people.

The initial chapters of the work, devoted to showing the reader how the old Testament came into being and how the Bible can be rightly regarded as the inerrant word of God, prepare the way for the ensuing chapters in which the author comes to grips with the meaning which the Old Testament has for the believer today. Yet these early chapters too, although at first glance they may not seem to be as directly related to the central theme underlying the work, are remarkable for the way in which they relate the books of the Old Testament to Christian faith. The first, a superb summary of contemporary biblical scholarship, relates the fascinating account of the way in which the Old Testament was formed; from it the reader will come to appreciate that the Old Testament is the heritage of a people led by God, a recital of God's saving deeds in history, constantly undergoing revision and reinterpretation until its culmination in the New Testament. The second chapter, which has been regarded by biblical scholars such as Roland Murphy as perhaps the most significant achievement of the entire volume, forces the reader to ask himself what he means when he says that he believes that the Bible is God's inerrant word, and in setting forth his views on this subject the author makes it quite clear that this position can be understood only by the man of faith who considers the Bible as a whole (both Old and New Testaments), as the developing, organic word of God operative in history.

The subsequent chapters of the book, "The Story of the Fall," "The Song of Victory at the Red (or Reed) Sea," "The Great Commandment," "Law and Grace," "Freedom and Repetition," and "Man Face to Face With Death," are outstanding examples of a biblical scholar motivated by pastoral zeal. For in these chapters the author puts his scholarly research to the service of God's people. His concern is, of course, to help modern readers of the Old Testament see how recent discoveries in archaeology, linguistics and allied disciplines shed light on the original meaning of the Old Testament narratives, but more importantly in these chapters he is at pains to help the Christian today see what makes the Old Testament his book. Throughout, Father Lohfink relates the thought of the Old Testament to the New; our understanding of Paul's message of justification through faith, for instance, will be immeasurably increased after a careful reading of the chapters given over to the great commandment and to law and grace. Perhaps the author's pastoral concern reaches its best in the final chapter of the volume, "Man Face to Face With Death." He shows how the attitude of Qoheleth (Ecclesiastes) in the Old Testament, for example, has close affinities to that of contemporary man, in whom belief and unbelief so frequently lie juxtaposed and who finds himself perplexed in a world of rapid social change.

In the original German the volume concluded with a chapter devoted to an appreciative study of Martin Buber's translation of the Bible. Since this study, however, can only be appreciated by those who speak German, it was thought advisable to omit the chapter from this English translation.

A remarkably lucid and penetrating volume, *The Christian Meaning of the Old Testament* ought to be of genuine spiritual and pastoral value to a wide range of the Christian faithful today.

# PREFACE TO THE GERMAN EDITION

However disparate the individual themes may seem to be in this volume, in fact the same question of the validity of the Old Testament is a thread running through the whole. At the beginning of my career as an Old Testament scholar, I thought I could best satisfy my hearers by bringing to the fore archaeology and the often astonishing new findings which it produces. It is true that there is always great interest in such matters. Nevertheless, I found in the course of time that other questions were more important to my hearers. I came to realize that these questions were very much my own. Our distance in time and culture from the Old Testament is great, and there is a powerful awareness of this at the present day, because of the feeling that we are once again at the threshold of a completely new era. As a result, the question constantly recurs of whether the Old Testament has anything to say to us at all. This feeling is not so strong with regard to the New Testament, although our remoteness from the New Testament is scarcely less. This shows that the question is ultimately a theological one. We are Christians, and live by the New Testament — does this not mean that the Old Testament is abrogated for us? This question cannot be answered by the methods of historical criticism which at present are the sole methods of exegesis. I must ask my fellow exegetes to understand this, if I sometimes consciously transgress limits which we are accustomed to observe in our academic work. On the other hand, everything depends upon not dismissing the question of the validity of the Old Testament by the hasty erection of a system which has all the answers. I have attempted to deal with this question in my chapter on the inerrancy of the Scripture. But for this very reason, I regard this chapter as extremely provisional. We must permit critical exegesis to say all that it has to say. We must return to it again and again for every text and for each new set of biblical statements. Consequently, those who are not scriptural exegetes, and who read this book, should regard it as an advantage that no particular abstract principle — such as "typology" — is laid down at the beginning, and is then applied in the same way to every case; but that instead the question of validity is posed in different terms in the case of the narrative of the fall and in the case of the song of victory in Exodus 15, and differently again for the Old Testament law and the existential philosophy of Qoheleth. Only when justice has been done to each individual statement, can it come to have a "Christian meaning" for us.

Norbert Lohfink, S.J.

# Contents

# THE CHRISTIAN MEANING OF
# THE OLD TESTAMENT

CHAPTER ONE

# THE FORMATION OF THE OLD TESTAMENT

In the field of theological scholarship, the problem of the formation of the Bible belongs to that branch of study known as "introduction." And in fact a "special introduction" inquires into the details of the formation of each separate book, outlines the history of the canon, and perhaps draws all this together into a survey of the history of the formation of the Bible as a whole. In the following pages, only a composite survey of this kind dealing with the Old Testament is given. Even this will still have to simplify and will not in any case be able to indicate what are hypotheses and matters of dispute. Apart from this, the formation of the Old Testament will be subjected to an inquiry from a very specific point of view. We must first make clear what this is.

## I. The Problem as It Affects the People of God

Almost all biblical studies which have in recent centuries brought confusion to the Christian Churches have originated in the field of study which is that of the special introduction. There is a reason for this. According to Christian belief, the formation of the books of the Bible is not simply a matter of history, it is also a theological issue. As a result the same reality falls within two fields of study. Conflicts between the two arise, and battle is joined. In the course of these disputes the lines of battle between the different views advanced by theologians and historians have repeatedly altered. Thus a retrospective glance over history may

1

be helpful in understanding the present awareness of the problem and the questions which seem appropriate to us.

## Starting Point: The Post-Medieval Situation

Even before historical sense awoke in the European mind, there were theological opinions concerning the authorship and the time and place of the formation of the books of the Bible. In the case of the Old Testament, practically all these opinions originated in ancient Judaism. The Church had accepted them from the synagogue without any real disagreement. Since they were of no significance for the exegetes of the Middle Ages, who were uninterested in historical considerations, they were merely an adornment, handed down rather mechanically, of theological education, interesting no one and provoking no reflection.

In addition — and tragic developments were to ensue later from this — they were inseparably entangled as a complex of Church tradition with the "doctrine of inspiration", and thus with theological statements concerning the divine origin of holy Scripture. The books of the Bible were thought of as documents composed by a few figures in the history of salvation, well known to us in other ways (Moses, the Prophets, King David and King Solomon, Peter and Paul, etc.), always as a single whole and under the influence of divine inspiration. The most extreme development of these views is probably the theory of "verbal inspiration" in seventeenth-century Protestant orthodoxy, which actually held the belief that the vowel signs and the accentuation of the original Hebrew text were divinely dictated.

## Scientific "Introduction" in Opposition to the Church

As the intellectual structure of European man was transformed and he was increasingly affected by historical considerations, traditional views concerning the formation of the books of the Bible also became the object of closer attention. They were taken seriously — but they were scrutinized as well. Following much preliminary work, particularly in the Catholic and Calvinist areas of France and the Netherlands, there arose in the areas of Lutheranism and the Enlightenment a scientific approach to the problems of biblical introduction which regarded itself as historical and critical. From the very first it was opposed to everything conventional and traditional in its field of study. Its scholars contradicted on an historical and critical basis almost every traditional thesis about the formation of the books of the Bible. Naturally the views of the historical and critical school themselves were soon severely disputed and underwent considerable changes. But, on the whole, we can say today that the historical and critical approach to biblical introduction was right, first in its new, scientific method, and second, in most of the theses which it advanced against traditional views which had been handed on unquestioned for thousands of years.

Unfortunately this was accompanied by a tragic error on both sides. Neither biblical critics nor churchmen were then in a position to distinguish, within the whole complex of traditional ideas about the divinely inspired composition of the sacred books, between dogmatic statements on inspiration and the many human concepts and traditions which were associated with them. Dogmatic authority was even ascribed to the old traditions of authorship. If they were abandoned—it was held—the divine origin of the Bible would no longer be tenable. When the champions of the new biblical criticism demonstrated the worthlessness of most of these traditions of authorship, they were bound to gain the impression at the same time that the divine inspiration of the Bible was also rejected. The new method became, in its early stages, a general attack on the traditional doctrine of inspiration. Churchmen saw no further than the academics: they accepted the field of dispute because they believed that they had to defend all the traditional opinions concerning the formation of the Bible, for the sake of the doctrine of inspiration. They constructed — with varying success in different churches — disciplinary barricades and ramparts.

In the Protestant Churches, though the battle was long and hard (as late as the end of the last century, Wellhausen gave up his chair of theology and had to become an Arabic scholar) the doctrine of inspiration largely fell by the wayside. Anyone who adheres to the doctrine of "verbal inspiration" today is looked down upon as a "fundamentalist" — above all in America. Otherwise, the word "inspiration" is used only in an essentially altered and weakened sense.

The same conflicts occurred in the Catholic Church, but they were stifled and concealed. They were, therefore, more protracted, and the outcome was different. Because this dispute was for the most part not conducted in public, many Catholics are still completely confounded by the outcome. Their surprise began when the 1943 papal encyclical *Divino afflante Spiritu* permitted historical criticism and, indeed, recommended it. It increased, when it became obvious that practically all Catholic exegetes had been waiting for the signal to begin immediately the intensive publication of historical and critical biblical studies, and to advocate in them very different theses from those so far tolerated within Catholicism. This process reached its peak when at the first session of the second Vatican Council, a majority of all Catholic bishops rejected the Curia's plan to restrict once again the freedom of the exegete, in order to restore so-called traditional opinions. How has this complete cessation of the battle with historical criticism within the Church come to be possible, when the Catholic Church is certainly not ready to sacrifice the doctrine of the inspiration of the sacred scriptures?

It came about through the gradual separation of the earlier concept of inspiration into its genuinely dogmatic and its purely human aspects. The genuine dogmatic doctrine of inspiration was then seen to consist of very abstract statements which, because of their very formal nature, left ample room for critical introductions to the Bible on an historical basis to study the human side of the formation of the Bible with the methods at their disposal. We cannot give a detailed account here of this more refined doctrine of inspiration. It must suffice to indicate the result. In Catholicism it is possible henceforth for the theological and dogmatic doctrine of inspiration and historical and critical study of the books of the Bible to be developed concurrently, without their creating difficulties for one another. It has become obvious indeed, that while they are both concerned with the same object, namely the formation of the books of the Bible, it is from different points of view in each case. The hatchet has been buried.

## The New Question: Is Collaboration Required?

Thus historical and critical inquiry into the formation of the Bible no longer has the militant, antiecclesiastical nature which it possessed at first. Its problems can be seriously posed, while at the same time a dogmatic doctrine of inspiration can be developed. But the mere existence side by side of these two disciplines raises a new question. Is historical and critical introduction to the Bible a branch of study which is in fact of no theological consequence? Naturally, it gives important assistance to the exegete in the details of exposition, as the essence of a text is more easily understood if one knows the circumstances of its composition. This, however, is of indirect value, not to be underestimated, but perhaps of more interest to the specialist exegete than the nonacademic reader of the Bible. "Special introductions" to individual books of the Bible seem to have no immediate direct theological relevance, so that they have no place, for example, in the preaching of the faith and in catechetics. The books of the Bible are significant for our faith only because they are the Word of God — and this is what the dogmatic doctrine of inspiration tells us. When, where, and how these books came into being may be of no consequence for our faith — and the same may be true of the historical criticism that casts light on these matters. The real problems of today for Catholic theology lie in the quest for the theological significance of the historical criticism of the Bible, whereas the shock caused by its existence belongs wholly to the past.

The medieval coupling of the doctrine of inspiration with specific concepts concerning the human side of the formation of the Bible is in a certain sense an essential theological requirement. If it is not made concrete, the dogmatic doctrine of inspiration is starved and becomes empty of meaning. Just as the methodological and theoretical separation between the two forms of inquiry into the origin of the scriptures was formerly necessary, so present circumstances equally demand that they combine their results in order to throw light on each other. Only from concrete knowledge concerning the human side of the formation of the Bible can the theological doctrine of inspiration achieve a living form, and only from an intelligent doctrine of inspiration can the introductory study of the Bible in terms of historical criticism obtain theological significance. But what shape will be taken by an attempt to combine these two disciplines, without destroying the characteristic nature which each discipline has come to possess?

This attempt is, in fact, already being made. Karl Rahner has sought, in his dogmatic study *The Inspiration of Scripture*, to make concrete the concept of inspiration. Even though it is scarcely expressed, a very close attention to recent exegesis and historical criticism underlies his arguments. Rahner considers the inspiration of the scriptures as given at the time when, in the primitive Church, God willed and effected, as the source and norm of her faith of later times, the scriptures as a constitutive element in the primitive Church, that is to say, as the objective reflection of its belief. In this definition, inspiration is no longer something freely floating in space, which may be conjured forth by God at any and every time or place, but rather is a reality which is very closely associated with the reality of the Church. "Scripture" comes from the Church, and comes about within and for the Church. This is in accordance with the conclusions of historical and critical study of the New Testament, which has shown more and more clearly that the New Testament was not given to the Church from outside, but grew up within her as the normal fruit of her life of faith. If Rahner's theory is right, then, conversely, it is true that when the historical critic describes the way the scripture proceeded from the Church, with the methods at his disposal, he is at the same time describing how God inspired the scripture. He is therefore making eminently theological assertions, even though their theological nature is legitimized not by his academic discipline itself, but by the dogmatic doctrine of inspiration.

Rahner is dealing principally with the problems of the New Testament. Yet his doctrine of inspiration also applies, *mutatis mutandis*, to the Old Testament. Here again, it becomes increasingly apparent from the historical criticism of the Old

Testament, that the Old Testament scriptures were not compiled by chance, but that they originated in the religious community of the Old Testament, and were required for vital functions within it, until the religious community of the New Testament adopted them as part of its own holy scriptures, as a fundamental element of its own prehistory. Dennis J. McCarthy, an American exegete who recently devoted an excellent study to the social aspects of the composition of the Old Testament, affirms at the conclusion of his argument that, in the course of his Old Testament research, he has come very near to Rahner's theory of the inspiration of the New Testament.

Assuming this new conception of inspiration, it is also true of the historical and critical study of the Old Testament, that its demonstration of how the books of the Bible are rooted in the "Church," at the same time gives a concrete interpretation of their inspired nature. If a description of the formation of the Old Testament lays particular emphasis on this aspect of the genesis of its books — as we intend to do in what follows, and as we are able to do, without being in any way disloyal to the principles of sound method — then it has a genuinely theological message to impart.

## II. *The Formation of the Old Testament*

Our survey must cover a period of more than a thousand years, from the Middle Bronze Age to the Hellenistic world civilization at the beginning of the present era. From wandering land-hungry nomadic tribes, under their sheiks — Abraham, Isaac, and Jacob — there emerged tillers of land; while world history paused for breath, the empire of David was created: a few centuries later the new Babylonian Empire swallowed up its last remnants and deported the inhabitants of Jerusalem to Mesopotamia, whence they returned under the Persians, and in the restored temple of Jerusalem founded the center of what was no longer a political but a religious structure which continued through the centuries as Judaism, partly in Palestine, and partly dispersed over the whole of the civilized world, till Jesus of Nazareth and the Church founded by him brought a crisis in its existence. Within this history of Israel the Old Testament was formed.

## The Period of the Patriarchs

In this epoch of the beginning of Israel, still largely obscure to us, one thing is clear: the Patriarchs claim to have had personal experience of God. They were led by the God whom they had experienced from their homeland in Upper Mesopotamia, and brought to Canaan, a land foreign to them, where they were promised posterity and possession of the land. They lived at a stage of the culture of their race which is still largely anterior to written records. Thus the knowledge of the Patriarchs' experiences of God, which are the enduring spiritual possession of their descendants, was handed down by the established techniques of an oral tradition, which is no longer known to us. They provide a reliable tradition, but the category they use is that of the individual saga, not the extended representation of history. The narrative material which is today collected in Genesis 12–50 was formed at that time and enriched over the centuries. The myths of prehistory which were later gathered together to form Genesis 1–11, such as the account of the flood, probably already belonged to the store of narrative possessed by these forefathers of Israel.

## The Covenant Between Yahweh and Israel

Some of the descendants of the Patriarchs were later in Egypt. The experience of being released from slavery and being led into the land promised to their fathers was seen by them as an act which was a revelation of Yahweh, their God. Moses and Joshua, the most prominent figures of that age, interpreted the revelation of God in word and in institutions. Israel chose as its form of organization the federation of the twelve tribes, and the enduring form of its relationship to God in a covenant. In an analogy to the secular treaty relationships, the covenant with God was thought of as a continuous treaty relationship between Yahweh and the people of Israel. Like every treaty, the purpose of the covenant with God was to give permanence to a relationship which existed at a given historical moment between the partners. In the worship of Israel, the saving action of Yahweh which had led to the covenant was continually proclaimed and recalled, and Israel pledged itself to carry out the demands made by the covenant with God. Thus the covenant with God was the distinctive characteristic of this religious community. Now, in the ancient Near East, a document was necessary for a treaty. No treaty was ever made without one. Two copies of the document were drawn up, deposited in the temples of the parties to the treaty, and then regularly read at public gatherings of the people. Similarly, a treaty document for the divine covenant between Yahweh and Israel must have existed at an early stage in Israel. It would be deposited in the sanctuary in the so-called Ark of the Covenant — both copies in fact, since it was a treaty with God and not with an earthly king. The document was regularly and ceremoniously read in the course of Israel's worship — perhaps within the framework of the great pilgrimage feasts. By the reading of the document, the people of God were kept aware of their origins and obligations. Should the occasion arise, official additions and extensions would be made to the document. The tradition preserved in Joshua 24 of the "assembly of the nation" at Shechem, shortly after the conquest of the land of Canaan, gives us an example of such a procedure. Through additions and extensions the treaty document grew considerably in the course of the centuries, and took on an increasingly complicated form. Yet however much it grew, it still remained the same document, which ensured Israel's contact with its origins, and formed one of its fundamental elements as a religious community.

Not only is this covenant document the first clear example in the history of Israel of written material which has later passed into our holy scriptures, but this piece of written material, the "covenant document," appears from the first in close association with the Old Testament religious community, growing out of it and actually helping to maintain its being through the course of history. It is even more intimately associated with the nature of the people of God than the holy scriptures of the New Testament were to be later, for despite its origin within and for the

Church, the latter is of a much more fortuitous and private nature than the "document" which is the whole basis of the relationship of the people of God to their God. On the other hand, this document is naturally not very comprehensive, and to understand it we must suppose the existence in Israel at the same time of broad parallel streams of tradition which lacked this formal and official character.

In the period of the Judges which followed that of the founding of Israel, the knowledge of revelation was handed down not only by means of the covenant document, but also, of course, by means of the widespread oral tradition which included the old sagas of the patriarchs and enriched them with much new material from the time of the Exodus from Egypt, the wanderings in the wilderness, the entry into the land of Canaan and the period of settled existence there. In the same manner the lyric tradition was cultivated. At the sanctuaries there was a set repertoire of sacral songs, and in families and villages there was an established tradition of folk songs and heroic odes. In local communities secular legal tradition was maintained, and in the sanctuaries sacral legal tradition, both of which were handed down orally in fixed formulae. All these oral forms of tradition also reflected, in the most varied ways, the religious understanding and the religious experiences of Israel. Yet at the same time the beginnings of written tradition were also appearing in the private sphere. In the age of the Judges the first collections of tales, songs, and legal material were already being made. Moses himself seems to have left some written material. Some collections from this period, such as perhaps the "Songs of Jashar" or the "Book of the Wars of Yahweh" (both are mentioned in the Bible), are no longer extant. Others may have been preserved in individual narrative cycles and in the legal material of the Pentateuch, in the Book of Joshua and the Book of Judges. But all this was more of a private nature. It had no official function in the people of God, such as the covenant document possessed. Nevertheless there were connections, and we must continue to pay attention to these records of the tradition as well, because at a later point we shall need to relate them closely to the whole community.

## David and Solomon; the Period of the Kings

With the advent of the monarchy, the cultural situation in Israel changed. This had certain consequences for the written and oral tradition.

Court life, the drawing together of an educated, accomplished class of officials, and the new and rising nobility demanded the introduction of the international system of education of the ancient East known as "wisdom." The wisdom education of Egypt and Mesopotamia soon influenced the upper classes and also reached down to the people. It took concrete form in collections of proverbs which were handed down in the schools of wisdom. King Solomon, the prototype of wisdom teaching in Israel, always appears as their author.

The consciousness of the importance of this particular moment in history, for the present and for posterity, led at court and in the temple to the setting up of archives and the keeping of annals. Naturally, in these collections of documents, a relationship to history and historical reality is expressed completely different from that in the legends from the periods of the patriarchs and the judges. Besides archives and annals, in the realm of literature, history writing began, though in a sense different from the modern idea of history. We still possess — worked into the books of Samuel and Kings in our Bible — an important record of the age of Solomon: the tale of the succession to the throne of David. The work tells how it came about that Solomon succeeded David, although he was not the oldest son. In this very first attempt, Israel reached a level in the literary presentation of history which had never been attained previously anywhere in the world, and which was not to be reached for a long time afterward. Besides such accounts of contemporary history, the extant sagas of folk memories of Israel, which had hitherto been handed down orally, were gathered together in historical works, planned on a large scale, one of which is still accessible to us to some extent, the so-called "Yahwist history," which now forms one strand of the Pentateuch, together with other works. It is called Yahwist because we do not know the author by name, and can distinguish him from other authors by the use in his account of the early history of the world of the divine name Yahweh. The Yahwist gathers together many traditions from the patriarchal age, the time of the Exodus from Egypt and the wandering in the wilderness, and from them constructs a single picture of history, on a large scale, which shows the dealings of God with his people. He precedes it by an account of the early days of the race, constructed from his reinterpretation of old traditions, running from the creation of the first man and his fall up to Abraham. By means of this the history of the people of Israel is given a framework in universal history.

So much for the new literary activity in the time of David and Solomon. The oral tradition continued to run parallel with it, and was also enriched by new productions. New poems and songs were used in the sphere of worship, after Jerusalem had also become the religious center of Israel, as a result of the transporting thither of the ark of the covenant, so that the cult developed to a completely new degree in the newly constructed temple. New rituals had to be created and new songs composed. New rites associated with the monarchy were instituted, such as the celebration of the enthronement of the king. For these, the royal psalms still extant in the Psalter were used — thus they did not originally refer to a king expected in the eschatological future, but to the "anointed" king who sat on the throne of David at any given time. The old forms of worship continued to exist alongside the new, and even for this period we have to assume that the old covenant document was used, venerated, and successively enlarged.

Was the basic relationship between the covenant document on the one hand and everything else on the other hand, which reflected Israel's consciousness of its faith, altered by all the new situations with regard to literature and the body of the traditional material? This cannot be maintained. In the sacred congregation, only the covenant document possessed a genuine official function. Nothing else can yet be referred to as "holy scripture" in the true sense.

When, after the death of Solomon, the nation was divided, the new situation with regard to literature and traditional material continued unchanged. A few examples may serve to illustrate this. The legends of the prophets, for example, that we read today in 2 Kings are examples of oral tradition, which was still growing at this time, and also provide examples of popular narrative form. They tell of Elijah, who, together with Elisha, came to be the ideal figure of the man of God. In the field of historical writing, there soon appeared in the Northern Kingdom a work which forms a parallel and a competition to the Yahwist historical work, which, because of the term it uses for God, is known to us as the "Elohist" history, and which is the second source of the Pentateuch. Perhaps the historical parts of the third source of our present Pentateuch, the so-called "priestly document," also came into being during the period of the kings. It is called the "priestly document" because it makes considerable use of professional priestly knowledge. In the sphere of the "wisdom" schools and educational practice, one important action is known to us from the Bible. King Hezekiah of Jerusalem (at the end of the eighth century) gave the order to gather together systematically the older collections of proverbs.

The covenant document itself continued to grow, as we may suppose, through additions and versions; also whole complexes of originally secular legal material were incorporated into it as divine law. In the time of King Manasseh, who apostatized to the Assyrian cults, it was lost. Under Josiah it was found again during some work in the temple, in 621 B.C. After consulting the prophets, Josiah ceremoniously renewed the old covenant institution for the whole nation, basing it on the old document. The account of this is given in 2 Kings 22 ff. Biblical scholars believe it is possible to deduce from this account that the new covenant based on the original covenant document which was then recovered is identical with the central part of the Book of Deuteronomy (that is, Deuteronomy 5–28).

The relationship between the original covenant document on the one hand, and all the other documentary and oral traditions in Israel on the other, continued to be the same as in the time of David.

## The Crisis of the Covenant: The Exile

From the apostasy of Manasseh it has already become clear that the religious history of the people of God during the period of the kings did not lack crises. This apostasy from belief in Yahweh was neither the only one, nor the first of its kind. Basically, through the increasing unfaithfulness of Israel, the covenant was coming to face an ever-growing crisis. This crisis was put into words by the prophets. They declared in the name of Yahweh that the covenant was threatened and finally broken, and proclaimed that the curse in the covenant, meant for the case in which the covenant was broken, would become effective, unless Israel retraced her steps. They interpreted in this sense the downfall of the Northern Kingdom, and the threatened exile in Babylon, which eventually came about, of the population of the Southern Kingdom.

The prophets originally delivered their message orally, and did not subsequently write it down. Many prophets are therefore completely unknown to us. We know the names of others, but not their prophecies. In the latter part of the period of the kings, however, the critical nature of the situation led to the beginning of written prophecy. Orally delivered prophecy was no longer valued, nor even listened to any more. Many prophets wrote their prophecies down, so that at least they would be there in later ages as evidence of the previous divine warning, and at the same time of the righteousness of God in venting his anger upon this people. Naturally, the prophets were not the direct authors of the books which we possess today under their names. First of all, single sentences and words were written down. These were later gathered together into small collections by the prophets themselves, or perhaps by their disciples, and as a third stage, the collation of all the collections and single texts which were the work of a certain prophet (and of his circle of disciples) produced the books of the prophets in our sense of the expression. This third stage usually took place after the death of the master. It may have taken centuries till the book of a prophet, which acted in some way as the esoteric fundamental text of a particular group within Israel, who were the "disciples" of the prophet concerned, was finally finished. We have only to consider the book of Isaiah, into which works of authors living two centuries after Isaiah were interpolated (Deutero-Isaiah and Trito-Isaiah). The prophecies of the founder of such a school of prophets were continually brought up to date by additions and adapted to new situations in Israel.

The books of the prophets therefore came into being as appeals aimed at the problems of the people of God, but at first they did not belong to the people of God as something officially accepted — the people in fact tended to reject their message. They were the carefully guarded property of small circles and groups, which were often actually in opposition to official religious practice, for the prophets and their disciples were above all great outsiders in Israel. Yet it was they who possessed the living seed of the future.

The apostasy of Israel and the catastrophe of the Babylonian exile were interpreted in another way, different from that of the prophets. Shortly after the beginning of the exile, an author unknown to us composed the "Deuteronomic history." It is meant to set out the history of the chosen people from their entry into Canaan up to the time they were driven from the land. The aim of the work is to explain the catastrophe which had occurred. Thus in it the history of seven centuries is examined from a single point of view, that of Israel's faithfulness and unfaithfulness to the covenant. The result of the examination is negative. Israel has sinned so gravely against its God, that God is justified in allowing disaster to fall upon the nation. There is only one thing the nation in exile can still do: repent, turn back to God, and hope for his forgiveness. We possess the whole of this historical work. It includes the books of Deuteronomy, Joshua, Judges, and 1 and 2 Samuel, 1 and 2 Kings, from our present Bible. At the beginning of the work, the covenant document of that time is included, in order to set forth at the start the standard by which Israel and her history will be judged. The ensuing historical account includes and adopts many of older documents, traditions, annals and archives. We have already mentioned them in detail in discussing the periods of the judges and the kings. They have been preserved for us by their inclusion in this comprehensive, historical work.

The "Deuteronomic history" is meant as a form of preaching in the situation of the exile, as an appeal to repent. We can neither prove nor deny that it was composed by official command. Yet the author would not have had the intention of creating a fundamental document for later generations of the people of God. He did not even know whether God would ever have mercy on his people. He has far less trust in God than the prophets of the same period, who change the tone of their preaching in the face of catastrophe, and promise Israel in its disaster a new and glorious saving action of God in the future.

## The Exile as a Break With Tradition: The Restoration and the "Holy Scripture"

The exile meant a break in the external form of Israel's tradition. Books and archives were destroyed in Jerusalem and Judah. More dangerous still was the fact that the normal handing down of doctrine in the temple, in schools and in families, was no longer functioning, because people had been uprooted.

In addition to this outward break in the tradition, there was a deeper one. The institution of the covenant was itself completely shattered. The destruction of the temple, the disappearance of the Ark of the Covenant, and the interruption of the cult of the covenant, were only external signs that the prophets had been right in foretelling the end of the covenant relationship between Yahweh and Israel. Of course, that God led the people from exile meant, according to the same prophets, that he had returned to his former faithfulness toward his people. But could the new institution which now came into being in Jerusalem at the restoration really be no more than the unbroken continuation of the old?

This is what the authorities of the nation, who carried out the restoration in the Persian period which was now beginning, may have asked. What did they do in the face of this double break with tradition, external and internal, in Israel?

In order not to let the break in the outward tradition become greater than it already was, they gathered together all existing traditions and tried to ensure their maintenance in the future.

This may perhaps have been done during the exile, but at the latest it was carried out at the moment of the return, at the beginning of the restoration. These precautions required that literary activity should be carried on under official auspices to a far greater extent than before, since the natural vehicles of tradition in the past were no longer available, or were no longer able to carry out their former task. In this way, therefore, traditions and literary productions in Israel, which previously had been "private" in a certain sense, were now taken into the official realm of the people of God.

In order to renew the internal tradition, that is, the covenant relationship with God, the attempt was made to give the newly-restored cult and the newly-formed community a structure similar to the former institution of the covenant. Thus it was also considered necessary to create a new "covenant document," or at least something that corresponded to the old covenant document.

Both tasks — that of a much more extensive writing down of religious traditions, under official auspices, and that of drawing up and regularly and solemnly reading a new covenant document — were associated in the creation, at that moment in history, of what we can call "holy scripture," in the familiar meaning of the term. The creation of this "holy scripture" was accomplished in several stages. These stages were of the nature of official acts, and took place at the instigation of those authorities in the people of God whose office was to conduct or supervise its worship.

First of all came the redaction of the *Torah* (we normally use the Greek name "Pentateuch"). The following task was undertaken: It was the intention to bring together in one work, first all the historical traditions from the earliest times up to the death of Moses, and second, all Israel's pre-exilic legal traditions. This plan was probably derived from the way in which the earlier covenant document had been drawn up, a document which had first narrated saving acts of Yahweh and then enumerated the obligations on the part of Israel which resulted therefrom. Thus, the Pentateuch also received, as its basic structural principle, the combination of history and law so typical of the Old Testament.

The following earlier literary entities were now gathered together in the Pentateuch. First, a series of narrative works — the Yahwist history, the Elohist history, and the priestly document. Second, a series of collections of laws — the "Book of the Covenant" (Exodus 20–23), the "Law of Holiness" (Leviticus 17–26) and Deuteronomy. The latter was taken from the Deuteronomic history, leaving those parts that the author of the history had added to the old covenant document. The priestly document provided the basic structure of the Pentateuch. To this basic foundation all kinds of individual narrative traditions and isolated laws were added, including in particular the cultic regulations for the worship in the temple.

Everything was put together in such a way that the reader of the present Pentateuch is led from the creation of the world through its early history, the history of the patriarchs, the liberation from Egypt and the wanderings in the desert, to Mount Sinai. There the covenant is made, and on this occasion most of the laws are proclaimed. Then the wandering in the wilderness continues, leading to the border of the promised land, where Moses once again repeats the law, represented in practice by the reading out of the covenant document of the later part of the period of the kings, which is contained in Deuteronomy. Thus the legal material is in part anachronistically back-dated to Sinai. Similarly, different traditions about the same events are often simply placed side by side or interwoven with each other. It is this which shows that the Pentateuch is a collation made in a later age and guided by a single idea, that of losing nothing that had been saved from the collapse of Israel, and which in one way or another reflected the more complete revealed knowledge possessed by later generations. If one starts with this assumption, the prevailing impression is not one of baroque intricacy, but of amazement that in spite of the nature of the work as a collection made at a late period, the element of the original and the monumental is still present in it.

The redaction of the Torah was followed at once by the second stage in the work of collection carried out by the founders of the community after the exile. The Torah, as the testimony of the origins of Israel, was supplemented by testimonies of faith from the time of the collapse of the covenant and the exile. These consist of writings from the different prophetic circles, and the Deuteronomic history. In the Jewish canon, this whole section is called simply "The Prophets." In the assembling of the prophets the Deuteronomic history was placed after the Torah. This was necessary principally because its first part, the Book of Deuteronomy, already had been used as the last part of the Pentateuch. Now it would be followed directly by the books of Joshua, Judges, 1 and 2 Samuel, and 1 and 2 Kings. Apart from this, the result of the joining of the Deuteronomic history directly to the Pentateuch was that there existed a continuous historical narrative from the creation of the world to the Babylonian exile. In Judaism, the books from Joshua to 2 Kings are called "The Former Prophets." In the old Jewish canon they are followed directly by the books of the "writing" prophets, first, the three major prophets, Isaiah, Jeremiah, and Ezekiel, and then the so-called "Book of the Twelve Prophets," which comprises the widely varying writings of the minor prophets. In Judaism, these were spoken of as "The Later Prophets."

The Torah, as well as the prophets in the above sense, were probably read in the temple and in the synagogues from the time of the restoration (even though this cannot be formally demonstrated). First came a reading from the Torah, then one from the Prophets. But song also had its part in worship. Thus a hymnal was created: the Psalter. It contained many songs, and indeed there were even whole collections of songs from the pre-exilic temple worship, but there also were more recent songs in it.

The Book of Psalms formed the starting point for the development of the third part of the holy scriptures of the Old Testament, which is called "the writings" in Judaism. This name is probably indicative of the fact that this part of the canon was not admitted for reading during worship (so that it is merely "scripture," and not a word repeatedly proclaimed abroad). Apart from this, the "writings" differ from other books current in Israel after the exile, in that they were added to the official canon of sacred books.

The writings grew in number in the course of the centuries.

It was really only the coming of Christ and the New Testament which brought an end to this growth of the third part of the canon.

## The "Writings"

When the crisis of the exile had been overcome, the need became evident to apply the newly gained insight to a new survey of the history of Israel. Here it was no longer necessary for it to appear as a radical break, as it did in the Deuteronomic history. Thus the Chronicler's history came to be written (1 and 2 Chronicles, Ezra, and Nehemiah). In it, history is traced from Adam to David by means of genealogies, and from David to the return from the exile by means of a continuous historical narrative (limited to Judah). There are also two appendices on the reforming activity of Ezra and Nehemiah. The author of the work is probably Ezra, the most important figure of the restoration. The work was intended to give the restored sacred community a new awareness of the history of salvation.

In the post-exilic community, the task was also begun of bringing the realm of wisdom education, which hitherto had no very close connection with the tradition of the covenant, within that of revealed faith. This was done, in what was still a very simple form, in the Book of Proverbs. At the head of a series of ancient collections of wisdom proverbs from the period of the kings a newly composed text is placed, in which a personified "Wisdom" appears, and is given a religious aspect. The synthesis goes further in the later, completely new, wisdom teaching of Jesus ben Sirach, and in the so-called Wisdom of Solomon, which belongs to the first century B.C. The figure of Wisdom is here identified with divine revelation, and indeed with the Torah. With the inclusion of these books in the third part of the canon, human teaching is basically related to divine revelation, and room is created for it to a certain extent within revelation. This also made it possible to bring in other valuable books from ancient Israel which had been preserved, although they were not immediate testimonies or documents of the revealed religion of Israel. Within the total context of the Old Testament canon they only bear witness to one thing; that as revelation takes place it sets free a space within human existence, without which human thought and feeling cannot develop freely. It is here above all that the Book of Job belongs. It takes the form of a philosophical dialogue on the problem of suffering in the world, which is enclosed within the framework of an old popular tale about the patience of Job, but which for the most part consists of a dispute on the problem in the form of polished speeches. The Book of Qoheleth, the Preacher, is a wisdom treatise on morality in human existence, and on submission to what God gives at any moment. The preacher may be called the existentialist of the Bible. On the other hand, it would be to misunderstand the book to describe its gentle melancholy as pessimism. It is more a treatise on the joys still possible for man. The Song of Songs is a collection of love songs, which must, however, be regarded not as folk-songs, but rather as highly-stylized poetry.

In the last centuries B.C. a new literary form developed which we call apocalyptic. The "apocalypses" were for the most part ascribed to a famous man of the past who is supposed to have received secret revelations from God and to have written them down in a book which had long remained hidden, which now (in the form of the same ancient book) was being made public. The apocalypses are for the most part visionary interpretations of history. The heroes of these theological novels have great visions concerning the course of world history, and afterward their symbolic aspects are explained by angels who interpret them. Of these apocalypses only one was accepted into the canon, one, moreover, which comes very early in the history of the category, the Book of Daniel. It professes to be the work of the prophet Daniel, who is supposed to have lived during the exile, but in fact it dates from the second century B.C. Its specific purpose, which is discernible behind a literary form foreign to us, but then quite popular, is the interpretation of the age at which it was composed in the light of the history of salvation.

In the second century B.C. there was once again a resurgence of historical awareness in Israel. The Jewish wars of liberation against several Hellenistic tyrants and religious persecutors led to the composition of a number of Books of the Maccabees, of which two were accepted into the canon.

The "Writings" are no longer all composed in Hebrew or Aramaic, for the later books are already written in Greek. The latter were probably never added to the canon in Palestine itself, but only in the Hellenistic diaspora Judaism from which they derived. Thus, in the last centuries B.C. a distinction gradually came into being between the Palestinian canon and that used in the wider Roman Empire. When the rapidly spreading primitive Church adopted the Old Testament as its holy scripture, it followed the wider Hellenistic canon of diaspora Judaism. There is a genuine continuity here. After the destruction of Jerusalem by Titus in 71 A.D., there came about the final separation between the Church and the synagogue. In order to make the dividing line as clear as possible, the Jewish canon of holy scripture was very strictly limited by the Jewish authorities at the synod of Jamnia at the end of the first century. All books not written in Hebrew were rejected, as well as Jesus ben Sirach, among those written in Hebrew. This is why the present-day Jewish Bible and the present-day Christian Old Testament differ in extent.

In rejecting the message of the New Testament, Judaism rejected not only the New Testament itself, but also a series of writings dating back before Christ, which in one part of Judaism at least had already come to be looked upon as canonical scriptures of the congregation of God. Luther and the other Reformers disregarded the Christian canon of the Old Testament and only recognized the Jewish canon as holy scripture (probably more out of a Renaissance enthusiasm for what was original than on account of genuine Reformation principles). In so doing, they basically assumed the existence of a gulf between the sacred community of the Old Testament and that of the New Testament. However, the Books of the Old Testament which were rejected by the Jews are printed in the Protestant version of the Bible as the "Apocrypha." The Hellenistic canon differed from the Palestinian not only in the number of books it accepted, but also in their arrangement. In Hellenistic Judaism, the "Writings" were placed between the Former and Later prophets. This arrangement is perhaps meant to underline the messianic prophecy found in many of the prophetic writings.

## A Summary

From the very first the Old Testament "Church" lived in accordance with a written document, which was one of its constituent elements. As the decisive factor in the formation of the Old Testament in its present form — which goes far beyond the extent of the old covenant document — we may point to the break with tradition caused by the Babylonian exile. It compelled the community to give wider scope to what was regarded as official scripture, so as to ensure the continuity of its faith and its life.

The continual growth of the covenant document before the exile, and of the Old Testament canon after the exile, makes a striking contrast to the composition of the New Testament, which was completed in a relatively short time, after which the Church possessed an unchangeable scripture as the document of its faith. As far as the Old Testament is concerned, the formation of the scripture was never brought to a conclusion in this way, either from the standpoint of the synod of Jamnia or of the Reformers. This is a reflection of the theological difference between the Old and New Testaments — both understood as saving ordinances. The Old Testament was anticipatory, still developing, still in the process of growing, still not finally certain of its goal. Thus its faith continually had to acquire a new certainty of itself in repeated additions and shifts of meaning within the documents in which it was expressed. As the scripture grew, the Old Testament "Church" grew toward Christ. In Christ, on the other hand, the final revelation of God has taken place. The end of time is present, and so the document of the faith of the primitive Church which was soon produced was eschatological, that is, final and unalterable. There may be in it a multiplicity of viewpoints (in New Testament terms, "theologies"). These "theologies" may build upon each other and thus be stages in a "development," as far as the history of ideas is concerned. Moreover, after the conclusion of the New Testament in the Church, there may be a development of its understanding, an actual "development of dogma." Nevertheless, it is true of the New Testament that it contains a fullness, and nothing can be added to it. On the other hand, the evolution and the openness of the Old Testament belong theologically to its essential nature.

# CHAPTER TWO

# THE INERRANCY OF SCRIPTURE

If it is necessary today to discuss the inerrancy of the Bible, it is not the idea itself which is under dispute, for this is an ancient and unequivocal tradition of faith. It can only be a matter of the understanding and formulation of this ancient belief. Sometimes the task is described thus: the older, abstract, deductive doctrine of inspiration must be transformed into a concrete and inductive doctrine of inspiration under the influence of our new knowledge of the Bible. It is true to say that the doctrine of inspiration held at the turn of the century was definitely too abstract and deductive. Yet there has never been a completely abstract, deductive doctrine of inspiration without a nucleus of concrete ideas. The formulae of theologians (and also of ecclesiastical documents) always offered, as an inevitable part of their content, a whole mass of concrete ideas which were held concerning the coming into being of the Bible at the time in question. It is, therefore, rather a matter of transposing a single religious truth, which can never be held in a chemically pure state, from an older, concrete doctrine of inspiration into a different, concrete doctrine of inspiration which must be constructed anew in accordance with our present understanding of the Bible. We are faced with a problem of language, which can be related to the task which John XXIII put before the Council and which the Council accepted, that of conveying the truth in pastoral language. Nor are we free to choose whether or not we wish to translate this ancient doctrine

24

into new terms. The limits of the understanding with which we encounter the Bible have moved outward, and are still doing so. They are increasingly defined, even for the laity, by the historical and critical study of the Bible. If one clings rigidly to old conceptions and formulae, there is a risk that they will spontaneously take on a new sense quite different from what was originally intended. If the ancient truth is to remain the same, we must ask whether we must not understand and formulate it differently in many respects.

In the attempt to reinterpret and re-express earlier statements, one must take care not to begin by watering them down. In other parts of dogmatic theology it may be wholly legitimate to advance a somewhat "negative" interpretation of inerrancy. Thus one may well designate the "faith" of the "ordinary, nameless Christian" as inerrant, where in the same consciousness error on a particular fact coexists with an openness, not related to a specific fact, to the full truth. But this conception is not satisfactory with regard to the Bible.

The doctrine to be accepted here is one of positive inerrancy on specific matters. For the inerrancy of the Bible results theologically from the fact that the Bible has God for its "author" and that it is therefore for us "revelation," "the word of God." But revelation implies the giving in positive and specific terms of the truth that is imparted, at least when it is a question of revelation in the form of "scripture." Otherwise revelation could never reach us who are the recipients of revelation. A Bible which erred in the specific matter of revelation could never be considered by us as the word of God, even if its human author was open to truth lying beyond his specific knowledge and statements.

The purpose of the following considerations is very modest. They are not intended to lead to radically new formulae, but for the most part only to exclude those among the traditional formulae which today inevitably lead to misunderstanding, and to commend the one which is still true today. This, of course, is not possible without an intensive study of the content of the concept of inerrancy itself.

In reading the patristic writers, medieval theologians and

modern treatises on inspiration, we can clearly see that the inerrancy of the Bible is predicated of three grammatical subjects: the Bible (as a whole), the books of the Bible, and the biblical writers (for which the technical term is "hagiographers" or "sacred writers"). The three ways of speaking of the matter are used simultaneously, the context deciding the choice. In the past century, however, the third mode was brought into the foreground. This happened in treatises on inspiration, as well as in ecclesiastical documents (which we should, in this case, consider not in so far as they state doctrine, but only as they reflect contemporary modes of thought and language — the problem of the exact subject of the statements concerning inerrancy was never subjected to analysis). One gets the impression that "the inerrancy of the sacred writers" is the precise expression, while "the inerrancy of the biblical books" or even "the inerrancy of the Bible" is loose terminology that is permissible but better avoided. This linguistic rule, as we hope to show in the pages that follow, adequately expressed the doctrine of the inerrancy of the Bible, within the scope of the ideas of the time concerning the composition of the Bible. The question remains whether it still does so within the scope of our present-day ideas. There is a suspicion that it is no longer in accord with reality, that it is abstract, and inapplicable and remote from the facts of the matter, and that if one attempts to apply it by force, it may even lead to error.

### Inerrant Writers or Inerrant Books?

How did theologians whose preferred view was that of the inerrancy of the sacred writers consider that the books of the Bible came into being? Their view was that the holy scriptures were the work of a small number of men. Moses had written the five books of Moses; Joshua, the Book of Joshua; Samuel, the Books of Samuel; Jeremiah, the Books of Kings, while the book of Jeremiah and Lamentations also derived from him. The Book of Isaiah was written by Isaiah; the Book of Ezekiel, by Ezekiel; the Psalms, by King David; Proverbs, Wisdom, Ecclesiastes and the Song of Songs by King Solomon. The same was true of the

New Testament. Eight sacred writers were supposed to have written its twenty-seven books. Anyone who doubts that these concrete ideas lay behind the encyclical *Providentissimus Deus* (the most important ecclesiastical document on the inerrancy of the Bible, 1893) has only to think of the much later decrees of the Biblical Commission on questions concerning the biblical writers. It is commonly acknowledged that the "Letter to Cardinal Suhard" (1948) and various official pronouncements of the Biblical Commission on the occasion of the second edition of the *Enchiridion Biblicum* (1954) enabled Catholic exegetes to depart, even in public pronouncements, from the theses on questions of biblical authorship which the Biblical Commission had propounded at the beginning of the century. To be sure, no one can say that *Providentissimus Deus* taught current theories concerning the composition of the Bible, but only that it presented its actual teaching within the limits of the language and thought of current theories. According to these theories, then, there was a small, easily identifiable group of inspired individuals. A sacred writer could have written several books (e.g. Solomon or Paul). But there was never more than one sacred writer behind an individual book. All books were composed as a whole and in their final form. To this extent it amounted to the same thing whether one said that the book did not err, or the author. The result was the same. Anyone who had reconstructed the original text, with the help of textual criticism, and who properly understood it, also understood at the same time what was being said by its single author.

The Church had taken over these theories about the composition of the Bible, without any real alteration, from ancient Judaism. Whether the latter, in allotting biblical books to definite persons, always understood authorship and the responsibility of a writer for his own work in our modern sense is perhaps debatable. But the nineteenth century, the age of the cult of Goethe and the veneration of the role of the creative author, was easily disposed to interpret the old traditions of authorship in this sense, going on either to oppose or defend them. When the Catholic doctrine of inspiration was worked out anew in the same century, it was psychologically inevitable that the emphasis should be laid, without further reflection, on the inerrancy of the sacred writers. That was the right and natural formulation of the doctrine of the infallibility of the Bible, with the limits of the understanding then possessed by Catholic dogmatic theology and Catholic churchmen, as well as by most exegetes.

In the meantime, the picture of the great writer-personality who wrote a work in one single draft has proved itself to be untenable in many cases. In the world of the ancient Near East it is the exception, and so it is in the Bible. The Pentateuch was worked on for fully 700 years, from Moses onward. Our books of the prophets were, before their acceptance into the canon, the sacred books of esoteric circles of disciples of the prophets, which were constantly being enlarged, commented upon and even altered with regard to their message.

The material of the gospels passed through a complicated formative process within the realm of the preaching of the primitive Church, before the synoptics formed their gospels from it. Thus the small group of well-known sacred writers is replaced by a large anonymous body whose outline is scarcely visible in the twilight of the distant past, and whose members cooperated as individuals on our sacred books. None of them achieved anything as complete as what was earlier attributed to individual sacred writers. But none of them was unimportant as regards the form and content of the final result.

What modification must be made in the former statements, if the formula of the "inerrancy of the sacred writers" was simply transferred unchanged into this new context? In the first place, more sacred writers were now postulated; second, their relationship to the books was now seen differently. It was accepted that God might have inspired several human collaborators, working either in parallel or succeeding each other. No single person was responsible for the whole book, and perhaps in carrying out their task most of them had not even any idea of what would emerge centuries later as the final product of the process of composition. Therefore the intention of what is said by individual sacred writers and what is in fact said by the books of the Bible were in many cases not the same. But these sacred writers were all supposed to be inerrant. The consequence was that in the light of the new knowledge, the old formula of the "inerrancy of the sacred writers" no longer meant the same as that of the "inerrancy of the books of the Bible," but far more. Not only the individual book in its final form and content had now to be considered as inerrant, but also every individual phase in its growth, a process which was admitted to be complicated and lengthy, for each stage corresponded to the intention of an "inerrant sacred writer" as he wrote. Each time the book was lengthened, added to, glossed, commented upon, combined with other texts or adapted to a new situation, a new and inerrant total statement of the book came into being. Each was piled upon its predecessor in the present canonical book like a stratum of an archaelogical excavation, and can be distinguished only through the scientific spectacles of the commentator. This would be the consequence of thoughtlessly combining the formula of the "inerrant sacred writers" with ideas based upon modern biblical knowledge.

We shall not discuss the fact that certain logical problems would be bound to arise here: the ideas contained in the strata laid one upon the other in the biblical books might well from time to time be contradictory (which need not imply the view that the inerrancy of the Bible is impossible, since it is the view that each of these strata is infallible which is under discussion here). Let us simply affirm that the religious tradition concerning the inerrancy of the Bible always refers to the completed books of the Bible as they now stand in the canon, and never to their previous history (unless the old concept of a "sacred writer" were to be applied to the direct production of the final form of the book). Thus in the light of our new knowledge of the way the scriptures come into being, the retention of the formula "the inerrancy of the sacred writers" at once takes on a new doctrinal content, which can be shown by the methods of positive theology to be different from its former doctrinal content. Moreover, the newly created part of the doctrinal content (the inerrancy of the early stages of the biblical books) possesses the property of automatically entailing a further series of new doctrinal statements. Anyone who regards the early stages of the biblical books as being free from error must in fact accept all the statements contained in them as the object of his belief as well. The results of the critical study of the early stages of individual books of the Bible would at once become an intrinsic element of dogmatic theology — a truly astonishing development, after centuries of struggle against the historical and critical study of the Bible.

It is therefore necessary to attempt to state the old truth in a new way, simply in order to maintain it as it was. Two ways of doing this are possible, and they are as follows.

One might simply regard the last man who had worked on a biblical book in the course of its gradual evolution as the "inspired author" in the sense understood by the doctrine of inspiration. All earlier stages in the book would then be characterized as "sources." Their authors would not be seen as having possessed the charisma of inspiration, and so there would be no valid reason for regarding them as inerrant. The old formula of "inerrant sacred writers" would consequently have to be changed into that of the inerrant final author. Once it was sufficiently established that by the "sacred writer" only the "final author" is meant, it would perhaps be possible to retain the old formula. This solution of the problem definitely does not contradict the positive doctrinal demand of ecclesiastical documents, although it departs in this from the underlying conceptions and from the language found, for example, in papal biblical encyclicals. One might nevertheless ask whether this solution does not somewhat neglect others who worked on a book of the Bible, and who did not have the good fortune to be the very last hand to touch it.

That is certainly not the case with the second possible solution, which we shall now describe. It is based on the idea that everyone who has made a real contribution to the wording and sense of a book of the Bible should be regarded as being infallibly guided by God with regard to the future book, that is to say, as being "inspired." One would then have to speak of a number of inspired authors, with regard to a book which came gradually into being. The inspiration of these authors, therefore, did not relate to their immediate work, considered in itself, but to that work insofar as it was directed by God, in wording and sense, toward the ultimate biblical book. Thus the inerrancy consequent upon the inspiration could not be predicated directly of all the individuals who worked on the book and their particular intention, but only upon the book which finally resulted. The inspiration of the many individuals whose work formed a book could then be regarded as a unity, which manifested its effect of inerrancy only once, in the final result of the collaboration.

With this "organic" solution, one could speak only of the "inerrancy" of a biblical book, and in certain circumstances perhaps, of the inerrancy of its final author, whereas one would have to avoid the formula of the "inerrant sacred writer" (unless one were to work out a new concept, such as that of indirect inerrancy). That the inspired authors possessed that negative inerrancy which consists in being open to (in the sense of not contradicting) the whole truth which still lay beyond them is in no way excluded by this view, but should in fact be postulated, for they are also vehicles of the process of revelation. One could hardly say that this attempt at a solution was not logically sound or that it was not compatible with a true understanding of the concept of inspiration. It does not detract in the slightest either from the influence of God or from the inerrancy of the final product (omnis sensus omniumque sententiarum of the books of the Bible, in the words of Spiritus Paraclitus, 1920).

The inner relationship of inspiration and inerrancy remains fully safeguarded. As with the first attempt at a solution, it necessarily departs from the underlying assumptions and from the language used in the older teaching documents of the Church, but it thereby safeguards their actual doctrine.

The difference between the two solutions worked out here does not lie in the fact that only one has dissociated itself from the way of thought and mode of expression of the old treatises on inspiration — they both do this. The distinction lies in the point at which the charisma of inspiration is seen to apply. Both solutions identify the inerrant meaning of the scripture with that of the final version of a book of the Bible. Both therefore satisfy present-day requirements with regard to statements concerning the inerrancy of the scriptures.

If despite this one asks which of the two theories should be preferred, an exegete would probably decide in favor of the second. In its assignment of inspiration to the authors concerned it is more in accord with the reality of the Bible than the first. A few examples may make this clear. In the Book of Ezekiel the main body of the text goes back to the prophet Ezekiel — according to the first theory, he would not have been inspired. The book was then put together as a biblical book by one of the first generation of Ezekiel's disciples, and he too would not have been inspired. Then on various occasions it was added to, glossed, and worked upon, and here too none of those who took part (except the last, who was responsible for no more than a hundredth part of the text proper) would have been inspired. Almost the whole of the actual text of the book would then consist, from the point of view of the theology of inspiration, of noninspired source material which the inspired sacred author had scarcely touched.

In the Book of Genesis, the Yahwist, the Elohist, and the priestly writer, who wrote the bulk of the present text, would not have been inspired, and Moses even less. Perhaps the redactor who combined the three sources was inspired. But perhaps it was a still later hand, who added still more and corrected the text. The authors of the messianic psalms, who understood their hymns to refer to the King of Jerusalem, and who had composed them for his enthronement and similar celebrations, would not have been inspired. The man who compiled the Psalter after the Babylonian exile would have been inspired, even though he possibly did not make a single alteration to the messianic psalms. For he intended them to be understood, in the context of the post-exilic books of hymns, of the eschatological Messiah, and so gave them a new meaning. In short, the limiting of inspiration of the "final author" very often makes those who carried out subsidiary work the principal figures, whereas the most important and influential biblical writers are not held to have charisma and inspiration. The main part of the biblical text would not have been written under the influence of God's inspiration, but would only subsequently have been regarded as unobjectionable by an inspired final author, and therefore taken into the book. The conceptions of extrinsic inspiration which the first Vatican Council rejected are indeed formally avoided here. But if it is definitely established as a matter of faith that God precisely guided the composition of our sacred books, then it is difficult to understand why he should not have guided the process of composition as a whole, and above all its main phases.

Yet whatever decision may be made between the two solutions, it seems advisable in any case to allow the formula of the "inerrancy of the sacred writers" to recede into the background, and, of the traditional formulae, to choose rather that of the "inerrancy of the books of the Bible."

### Inerrant Books or an Inerrant Bible?

Of the three traditional formulae, we cannot be satisfied with the result achieved so far. There are still two to choose from. There is a consideration which compels us to pose further questions. Hitherto, the terms "final author" and "final sense of a biblical book" were treated as established and familiar entities. This, however, is no longer so. In the definition of the relationship between "the books of the Bible" and the Bible as a whole, our conception has altered here again as a result of the products of historical and critical scholarship. The separate "biblical books" are now studied with regard to their nature as books. This, too, has naturally affected the object of the concept of biblical inerrancy. First, let us consider once again the framework of the understanding of earlier generations, and try to see how they could legitimately assert the biblical inerrancy of every individual book. The theory was that each of the outstanding personalities who were the sacred writers has written his book (or his books) at a given time. Once such a book had been composed, it was published, and once it was made public, then it was a fixed, unchangeable entity — as was the case with books in the nineteenth century. The books of the Bible were at some time or other gathered together and entered in a catalog, called the "canon." But this procedure remained external to the books. When a nineteenth-century academic bought himself a bookcase and gradually put more and more books into it, at the same time not forgetting to enter them carefully into a catalog, all these books stood on the same shelves, but each remained an entity in itself. Whenever a book was added, or another taken away, no part of the total meaning or of the statements contained in the other books which stood on the shelves was altered. Thus, according to the views of that period, books of the Bible which already had been accepted into the canon remained the same when another book was taken into the canon. They said exactly the same thing as before. They had long received their final form.

The holy scripture was scarcely ever regarded as a unity and a whole. When this was done, attention was directed to the external entity assured by the Church, the catalog of the canon, or else an immediate leap was made into the transcendent and reference made to the divine author who had given all the books, and was thus the cause of the impossibility of any contradiction in any of the books. There was never any discussion of a fundamental unity inherent in the Bible itself. It was axiomatic that every book stood on its own and was inerrant in itself. This meant that in dogmatic theology, even in giving a "scriptural proof," one could use every book of the Bible, either of the Old or New Testament, with equal legitimacy, with the exception provided by a few relics of a different view, which derived from the patristic period or even from the New Testament, and which, for example, regarded the laws of the Old Testament as largely abrogated. But in general, every book of the Bible stood on its own, and there was no external corrective to it. Each book of the Bible was seen simply as adding something more to what was in the others.

This static conception of the canon has undergone a crisis. Even the compilation of the canon is increasingly seen, from the point of view of historical criticism, as an evolutionary process. The boundary between the history of the formation of individual books and the history of the canon becomes less distinct. The growth of the canon seems to be no more than a further stage, somewhat different in form, of the process which brought the individual books into being. In our present inquiry we are not looking so much at the history of the New Testament canon, but principally at the gradual building up of the canon of the Old Testament, and second at its incorporation into a New Testament framework. In this context, the process by which the canon came into being after the exile seems simply to have continued the process by which individual books were composed before the exile, as far as we can understand that process. One layer of meaning was laid upon another, and new texts which were added led to an increasingly comprehensive texture of meaning. Between the alternation and interweaving of the Yawhist, Elohist, and priestly writings within a single "book," and the alternation and juxtaposition of the historical works of the Deuteronomist and the Chronicler within the "canon" there is no real practical difference. In both cases different versions of history are associated, complement and correct each other, and constitute together a new and higher unity of utterance. The same is true, within the canon, of the wisdom books. They complement and criticize each other, and at the same time, as a unity within an even greater whole, they form a counterpoint to the Torah and the prophets.

The essential point in this phenomenon is that this unity of the canon was consciously sought. Those who composed and used the canon never regarded the individual "books" in the philosophical sense as books, that is, as bodies of meaning, complete in themselves. In this sense, they only regarded the canon as a whole as a book.

This has become increasingly clear in recent years, particularly through the fact that scholars have paid closer attention to the late glosses and additions to the books of the Bible. This filigree work carried out upon the text of the Old Testament at a late period, overlapping that of the formation of the canon, in fact reveals a mentality which regarded all the books of the canon as related to one another. It was assumed that all the books of the scripture illustrated each other. They shared the feeling which guided Martin Buber in his translations, the sense of the Bible as a single book, in which everything draws its life from all the rest. Thus, for example, in the latest additions to the book of

Deuteronomy (Dt 4:25–31 and 30:1–10), the ancient concept of the covenant, which is characteristic of the theology of the whole Pentateuch, is illuminated by the prophetic preaching of the future new covenant. But this means that books such as Isaiah, Jeremiah, and Ezekiel, which came much later into the canon, could be regarded as critical principles which could be applied to utterances of the Pentateuch. This means that the Torah and the prophets were regarded as a single complex of meaning. The study of these late passages in the Old Testament has only just begun, and much remains to be done before it is satisfactorily completed. The late additions and glosses for the most part consist of cross-references — sometimes only within the book itself, but often from outside the book — to other books of the Bible. This shows that no book of the Bible was read except through the *analogia scripturae* — within the unity of meaning of the whole scripture.

Thus the canon was not regarded as an outward collection of individual books complete in themselves, but as a single book. When this book grew through an addition to the content of the canon, the total statement made by older parts of the canon was bound to be altered and set in a slightly different light. Like the separate processes leading to the formation of most of the books of the Old Testament, the history of the canon itself is a further testimony to the attitude to tradition, both conservative and liberal at the same time, which was characteristic of ancient Israel: no word had to be lost, no phrase allowed to fall to the ground — at the same time everything was in constant movement, and what already existed was constantly set in a new light, everything was taken up and carried along the road to new goals known only to God. If a book was in the canon, its wording was taboo; apart from minor additions and glosses no further changes were made. But this was true of its wording, not of the totality of its utterance. This was necessarily changed by each new text taken into the canon. Thus the whole canon was constantly moving toward its total meaning.

Our modern concepts of literary authorship are of no use to us here. But in our dogmatic theory of holy scripture, ought we to be bound by modern sociological structures? If we attempt to free ourselves from them and to adopt a more fundamental standpoint, we cannot help but include this transformation of the utterance of books whose wording was already fixed, a process implied by the growth of the canon and carried out with conscious intent, within the concept of "authorship," from the theological point of view. Consequently, the taking up of a new book into the canon was, among other things, an "act of authorship," both with regard to the book itself, and also with regard to the books already in the canon, and therefore to the Bible as a whole. In the sense of the doctrine of inspiration, at least in the form of the "organic conception" which we preferred, we are bound to postulate the charisma of inspiration for this act. If in the first part of our study the "final author" and the final result of the process of "formation" of the books of the Bible was of particular importance, it now appears that as long as the Old Testament canon continued to grow, no single book within this canon had yet found its final author and its ultimate meaning.

At some point, however, the growth of the canon came to an end. At a certain point in history a decision which was the equivalent of an act of authorship was made, in the sense that the Old Testament was to remain as it then was, its statements were to be final and authoritative, and it was to be regarded as a complete book. The point at which this decision was made can be specified. It is the moment when the Old Testament as such was taken into the New Testament. We mean here by the "New Testament" not the collection of New Testament books, which was still to have its own history, but the reality itself which is reflected in these books. Jesus, the apostles and the primitive Church made, with regard to the Jewish canon which they found before them, the decision that that Old Testament canon should form the enduring background history and document of the New Testament which had come in Christ.

By virtue of this decision a further and final addition was at once made to the Old Testament, that of the New Testament in the form of the books which were either already available or were still to come, but which never in their content went beyond the fact of Christ. Like every previous addition, this once again changed the pattern of meaning in the Old Testament as a whole. Thus, to use paradoxical language, one could say that in the sense of the dogmatic doctrine of inspiration the New Testament was one of the "sacred writers" of the Old Testament.

It is, of course, the last sacred writer. For this addition is the last which was made to the Old Testament. Jesus and the primitive Church knew that the end of time had come in Jesus. The process of revelation itself had come to an end in him. It was their conviction that after the utterance of Christ no new and determinately decisive element could be added to the significance of the Old Testament. The developments which are visible within the books of the New Testament were essentially of a much more limited nature than what had taken place hitherto. They only set out the fact of Christ, and never go beyond it. After Jesus Christ no word of God would be given to supersede him, for he is the word of God in the full sense. Thus in him the development of the meaning of the Old Testament had to come to a halt.

These affirmations are in accordance with our faith. It is not this, however, with which we are concerned; what is of decisive importance for our present concern is that they describe the intention of Christ, of the apostles and of the primitive Church with regard to the Old Testament. The fact of Christ is like the key signature at the beginning of the score which determines everything that follows. The New Testament bears constant witness to this. We are not discussing here the primitive Christian exegesis of individual passages and the methods it employs. In this, Jesus and the sacred writers of the New Testament were also children of their time. What is of decisive importance is the basic christological intention with which they read the Old Testament. This is a decision which is equivalent to an act of authorship. It affects not only the individual passages of the Old Testament which are cited and interpreted within the New Testament, but the Old Testament as a whole. It makes a single book of the Old and New Testaments, not merely from the point of view of their transcendental divine author, but also with regard to its inherent purpose, an intentionally unified body of meaning, which is very complicated and manifold, but which cannot be broken up into independent parts. Only within this all-embracing unity is the sense of each individual statement finally determined.

It is only here, with the unity of the whole scripture, that we have reached the point where biblical inerrancy can be meaningfully asserted. Each previous and more fragmentary picture is called into question by our knowledge of the intentions which guided the evolution of the canon. It is here alone that we can find the sense intended by the holy scripture as it is given to us by the Church, and to which in consequence the doctrine of biblical inerrancy refers. All that proceeded this was merely preliminary matter.

If the conclusion had been reached from the first part of this study that only the "final authors" of biblical texts are inspired, then to be consistent we would have to say that the sole inspired "author" of the Old Testament was Jesus, and certain figures of the primitive Church. This is not a very convincing statement, and therefore we must finally set aside the solution which limits inspiration to the "final author." In the sense of the second, "organic," solution the process of inspiration begins deep in the Old Testament, but extends (even for the Old Testament itself) into the New Testament, and its ultimate goal is that of a single "book," the Bible.

Of the three formulae which tradition offers for biblical inerrancy, we saw in the first part of this study that the "inerrancy of the sacred writers" was inadequate in the framework of our new knowledge of the composition of the Bible, and that of the "inerrancy of the books of the Bible" is now also seen to be inaccurate. On the other hand, the third ancient formula, that of the "inerrancy of the Bible," can be maintained. Thus the demand for a language which is of pastoral value can be fulfilled in the case of the inerrancy of the Bible, without looking for a radically new mode of speech. It is sufficient to choose the most appropriate from possible forms of language which already exist and are sanctified by long usage.

## Prospects and Limits

We have been concerned only with a linguistic problem. We asked which formula threatens and which promotes a proper understanding at the present day of the ancient doctrine of the inerrancy of the Bible. It was not possible to answer this question without a fundamental rethinking of the question of inerrancy. The situation imposed upon us lines of thought which in part at least were new. To think new thoughts is always a risk. We would explicitly emphasize that our study does not intend to be anything more than tentative, and is presented here with all necessary caution.

Precisely because of its novelty, the picture we have set forth could easily be liable to misunderstanding and misinterpretation. It therefore seems advisable to conclude by drawing certain consequences, and to define the limits of our view in various directions.

1. The statement that the Bible is inerrant only as a unity and as a whole must not be understood in a minimalist sense. The whole comprehends and supports individual parts. In the structure of the whole each book and each sentence, and even all the layers of meaning piled one upon the other in the course of history, naturally share in the inerrancy of the Bible. The degree to which they share in it is measured by the degree to which within the whole pattern of the meaning of the scripture they contribute to the formation of its total statement. In this sense it is both possible and obligatory to say that *every statement of the Bible* is inerrant. But in this sense alone! If it is true as a general philosophical and epistemological principle that the meaning of a statement can never be established apart from the whole system of reference within which it stands, then in the realm of the Christian treatment of the scripture, this system of reference is always the whole scripture, even with regard to statements in the Old Testament — and this is in fact the intention of the scripture itself. Consequently, biblical inerrancy itself can be asserted only of the meaning established in this way.

Once a word, a sentence, or a book is taken out of its context in the whole of the scripture and isolated in itself (being perhaps still related to its time and environment in the history of thought, but not, however, related to the scripture as a whole) there is no longer any guarantee of its inerrancy. Anyone who uses the methods of historical exegesis to dissect an older layer of meaning from the Bible and consciously refuses to place it in its proper position in the total statement of the scripture from the point of view of the event of Christ, may perhaps be carrying out a brilliant piece of academic work, indispensable in the context of exegesis as a whole; but he cannot lay claim without qualification to inerrancy for the utterance that results.

The question, of course, ought to be posed (within the framework of the very neglected dogmatic tract, *De oeconomia Veteris Testamenti*) concerning the function which the scripture had for the men of the Old Testament, and whether and to what degree "inerrancy" was predicated of it in that context. But in fact it does not seem so certain that the "old covenant" was based upon the scripture as the "source of belief" in the same way as the "new covenant," and that the "scripture" which from the time of the exile on became important in Judaism should be considered theologically to have had exactly the same function at that time as the function of the scripture in the New Testament community.

This question bears comparison with the completely open and parallel question, whether an "infallible" teaching office existed before Christ. In any case, it is not possible to claim inerrancy for a transitory layer of meaning in the Old Testament in the name of the Christian doctrine of the inerrancy of the Christian Bible. When Paul says that only the "spirit" (the gospel of Christ) gives life, whereas the "letter" (the Old Testament read apart from Christ) kills (2 Cor 3:6), he qualifies this immediately by saying that even the "dispensation of death . . . in letters" came in "splendor" (3:7); but is it immediately evident that we must also accord to this "splendor" inerrancy in our whole sense of the word? Perhaps it is not possible to get any further by means of a theological and deductive approach in this question, and it would be better to attempt a solution simply from the results of the concrete scientific study of the Bible. If this shows that even where, with regard to many transitory layers of meaning in the Old Testament, all the normal hermeneutic rules have been applied (e.g. that of paying close attention to the literary category used and the statements the author intended to make), statements remain in individual cases which one can only term "errors" from an historical or theological point of view, then one must perhaps abandon the idea of the inerrancy, within the Old Testament itself, of the early stages of the Bible. But, as we have said, this is something which no longer belongs within the context of a Christian doctrine of inspiration, which is concerned with the Christian scripture as it is set out in the canon of Trent; rather it is the concern of the dogmatic tract, *De oeconomia Veteris Testamenti*, which has lain fallow for centuries. When modern exegetes come up against "problems of inerrancy" in the Old Testament, these problems are normally concerned with such transitory layers of meaning in the Old Testament.

2. In this context we must say something about the concept of the *literal sense*. Modern biblical scholarship, working with historical and critical methods, is increasingly establishing the usage in which the term "the literal sense" applies to the sense obtainable by these methods. In dealing with Old Testament texts, this "literal sense" is invariably located in the realm which has just been described by the concept of "transitory layers of meaning in the Old Testament." In this case the "literal sense" of the Old Testament falls into the sphere described by Paul as the "letter." This modern usage, which in a wholly unexpected way brings us back to Pauline terminology, is the sense in which even the encyclical *Divino afflante Spiritu* understands the concept in one passage, where it opposes the "literal sense" to the "spiritual sense." But this understanding of the concept is not identical with that which was usual in recent centuries in Catholic theology, and which was normally assumed in ecclesiastical documents, even, apparently, in *Divino afflante Spiritu*.

This "theological" concept of the literal sense was formed above all by Thomas Aquinas. For him, the intention of a particular sacred writer in making the statements was of no account. By the literal sense he meant the sense of the biblical text itself, and contrasted it with the meaning of the things and events with which the biblical text deals. This is a completely different point of view from that of Paul, or of the present day. This "theological" literal sense means nothing other than the meaning of the scripture read as a whole and in the *analogia fidei*. When theological tradition refers to the "literal sense" as inerrant, it is always assuming this "theological" understanding of the concept. Assuming the older conceptions of the coming into being of the books of the Bible, these niceties in the definition of the concept of the "literal sense" are relatively unimportant; for from that point of view there were, for example, no tensions between transitory and final layers of meaning in the Old Testament. But in our present-day assumptions, by contrast, much depends upon the concept of the "literal sense" with which the tradition of recent centuries and the Church's magisterium link the doctrine of the inerrancy of the Bible. It ought not to be possible to demonstrate that inerrancy is associated in the Church's doctrine with a "literal sense" defined purely in terms of historical and critical method, which does not represent the ultimate utterance of the Bible.

3. A consequence of the change in the concept of the "literal sense" is the modern idea that in the scripture there is also a *fuller sense* of Old Testament utterances, which goes beyond the consciousness of the original author. In part this is only an attempt to justify the traditional interpretation of the prophetic texts, and especially of the *Protoevangelium* of Genesis 3:15; but to some extent a significant hermeneutic method for reading the Old Testament in the light of the New has been developed. This is wholly in accord with the ideas set forth in this article. But it has been assumed without discussion that even the transitory layers of meaning within the Old Testament contain inerrant scriptural statements, and the "fuller sense" has often been defined as the sole "meaning of the divine author" in a way which is scarcely reconcilable with the basic principle of the Catholic doctrine of inspiration. By contrast with this, it seems possible and indeed necessary to us to understand the reading of the Old

Testament in the light of the New as the sense of scripture intended not merely by God, but also, in a sense both inherent in the Bible and in terms of the positive study of the Bible as it took shape in the world, intended also by human "authors," since it is the sense intended by the final (New Testament) author of the Old Testament.

4. The general view presented here is not so close to the theory of the "fuller sense," which is speculative and doubtful in many respects, as to the basic hermeneutic principle of the patristic period and medieval theology, the doctrine of the *spiritual sense* of the scripture. Naturally, in making this comparison, we do not have in mind individual techniques of exegesis, particularly the passionate delight in allegory, that was the fashion of the time. All that is important is the basic hermeneutic principle. Henri de Lubac has described it for us in a work of several volumes. Its starting point was the Pauline distinction between "letter" and "spirit." The "letter," also called *historia*, is the sense of the Old Testament which Old Testament authors gave it in their historical situation. The "spirit," also called *allegoria* (and often further subdivided into *allegoria, tropologia* and *anagogia*: hence the "doctrine of the four-fold sense of scripture"), is the New Testament, that is the Gospel of Christ, and with regard to the Old Testament a christological reading of it.

The synagogue, which did not accept the Gospel of Christ, knows only the "letter" and therefore the "veil of Moses lies over their hearts" (2 Cor 3:15). The synagogue concluded its canon before Christ came, and refused the acceptance of the New Testament books into it. The Church, however, added the New Testament, and on this basis alone, that is, on the basis of Christ, reads the whole Bible as a unity. But the Lord is the Spirit. Consequently, in its christological interpretation the Church possesses the "spiritual sense" of the Old Testament. The Fathers and the medieval theologians often make use of the miracle of Cana as an image of this. Just as the Lord turned the water in the jars into wine, so he has changed the literal sense of the Old Testament into the spiritual sense. The scriptural exegete has naturally always to begin with the *historia*. But he must pass on as soon as possible to the *allegoria*, for it is only this which provides the true nourishment of the word of God.

Ancient exegesis, of course, still had no sense of the often complicated layers of meaning which already exist within the Old Testament itself. In order to distinguish them, the methodical scholarship of modern exegesis was necessary. But the step forward in the development of its meaning which was decisive in the framework of the whole Bible, the inclusion of the Old Testament canon in that of the New Testament, was clearly set out by classic Catholic exegesis, in strict accord with the way in which the New Testament understood itself, and was made the basic principle of scriptural exegesis. We must once again be prepared to learn from it.

5. Even in recent times, and despite all the theories of the dogmatic tracts on hermeneutics, *the practical use made of the Old Testament* has probably never really departed from the ancient hermeneutic principle of the spiritual sense, and has thereby implicitly always maintained the thesis developed here of the inerrancy of the Bible as a unity and as a whole.

The view always maintained in dogmatic and, above all, in moral theology, that the greater part of the old law has been abrogated, can basically only be justified when one takes the scripture as a whole and regards what was intended in the statements of the Old Testament lawgivers as being already brought into question by the New Testament.

That the scripture should be regarded as inerrant only as a unity is also assumed in the way in which the "holy war" of ancient Israel, the "cursing psalms," the concentration of Old Testament religion on the present world, and similar phenomena are evaluated. The study of literary categories is of use here only in marginal cases. The concepts and statements which give offense form for the most part the central intention of the statements of the authors within the terms of the Old Testament itself. But it is customary to speak simply of the provisional nature of the Old Testament revelation, and to regard the original statements as relative from the point of view of the New Testament. Cardinals even demanded in the Council debates that the "cursing psalms" be excluded from the breviary. But if, for example, the Book of Ecclesiastes was inerrant in the exact meaning intended by its original author, without regard for the whole body of scripture, and for the New Testament in particular, then one would have to regard the preacher's doubt about a world to come, and his existential philosophy, which is based upon his radical awareness of death, as wholly inerrant and binding.

Even the tracts on hermeneutics which are normally in use observe, in their discussion of such problems, that the texts of the Bible must naturally be read in the light of tradition or of the faith of the Church. Are they not aware that by so doing they have already abandoned in many cases the view that in the Old Testament it is the original sense which is inerrant? Or do they wish to assert in every case that it is the historical and critical interpretation of the text which is in error, and that, for example, Qoheleth sought throughout to say what critical scholars have only found in later books of the Old Testament and in the New Testament? We hope not; for this would imply a mistrust of modern methods of biblical scholarship which since *Divino afflante Spiritu* is hardly permissible. Thus the position is probable that in the final issue exegetes, without being fully aware of the fact, already hold the view that the scripture is only inerrant when it is read as a unity, and when individual statements are critically related to the whole. Such a critical treatment of individual statements is far from meaning that they are wholly rejected, but rather that they are restored to a real significance in the light of the whole. One may ask whether by removing "cursing psalms" from the breviary, one might not be throwing out the baby with the bath water.

The acuteness of these hermeneutic problems is often obscured at the present day by all that is said about literary categories. One sometimes gains the impression that all difficulties concerning the inerrancy of the Bible could be resolved by a closer analysis of literary categories. This, however, is not the case. Form criticism is extraordinarily important in order to come to grips with the meaning originally possessed by the text. A large number of apparent problems — especially with regard to statements concerning natural science and history — are solved incidentally when this method is applied for the purposes for which it is in any case necessary. As an organic component of the method of literary criticism, it is indispensable to modern exegesis.

Pius XII earned the thanks of all exegetes by setting this forth so clearly in *Divino afflante Spiritu*. Since there are still circles which are not prepared to realize this, one can only be glad that the Council was led to emphasize the legitimacy of form criticism; but this does not prevent us from pointing out its limitations. It is not a panacea. Among Catholics in particular, statements are sometimes made in the name of form criticism which it does not justify. An example of this is the creation text in Genesis 1. It has been said that on the basis of its literary category, this text is only concerned with a single statement, that God created everything. Anyone who is making a judicious use of form criticism would probably be more cautious here. Does not the category here also intend to imply a further statement with regard to the creation itself, its structure and construction? The statement that Genesis 1 is merely concerned to state the fact of the creation is only true within the horizon of the Bible as a whole. There different world views are juxtaposed and render each other more relative. On the basis of the principal emphasis of the Gospel as they are laid down in the New Testament, it is in fact only the statement that God created everything which is at issue, so that one can rightly regard this alone as inerrant, and not also the statements which describe the form of the universe in Genesis 1.

A further example may be found in Joshua 6–8, the narrative of the destruction of the cities of Jericho and Ai by Joshua. According to the findings of present-day archaeology, Joshua can hardly have destroyed these cities, for in the period in which he lived they had already been in ruin for several centuries. Can one then wriggle out of this by referring to the literary category of these chapters, to the character of "legend" and "heroic saga" which they possess? Even legends and sagas normally possess an historical kernel, and in this case, once all the individual narrative details have been removed, it is presumably the fact of the conquest of the city by Joshua. At least one must accept that the Deuteronomist included this chapter in his history only because he intended to state that Joshua conquered these cities — though he may very well have been aware of the nature of the stories in their concrete form as legends and sagas. Thus the tensions between these narratives and the findings of archaeology cannot be removed simply by determining their literary category.

It is another question, however, whether in the whole context of the biblical message, where it is no longer the "land" which forms God's real saving gift, the details of the Israelite conquest of Palestine are not so marginal that they can be neglected, and whether the statement concerning the history of salvation, that Yahweh gave his people the land promised to the fathers, is the only one that can be claimed to be inerrant. These two examples must suffice. It would be possible to replace them by others similar in pattern, if anyone felt unable to accept these particular examples on detailed exegetical grounds. They are only meant to demonstrate one thing: that at the present day hermeneutic solutions are often put forward in the name of form criticism which in reality are based upon our thesis of the unity of the scripture.

Thus our thesis does not seem so novel after all, but is merely a conscious retrospective statement of what fundamentally has already been the practice.

6. *Purely historical exegesis*, as is now carried out at the present day with such vigor, is in no sense rejected by our thesis. It is an irreplaceable necessity, as the initial and transitional phase of the process of exegesis. Even the ancients always began with the *historia*, before they passed on to the *allegoria*. Nor is the understanding of the scripture as a unity simply an unhistorical theory imposed upon the Bible, a matter of pure dogmatics. Rather, as we have tried to show, it can be verified in terms of historical criticism as a phenomenon inherent in the Bible. Of course, from the historical and critical point of view, one could adopt only the basic principle of the New Testament view, that is, that the whole scripture must be understood through Christ. In the exegesis of individual Old Testament texts, one would

adopt this New Testament point of view, but as far as details are concerned one would attempt to understand the "total sense" of Old Testament texts by actually applying present-day methods of understanding. How far such a process can be called one of historical criticism is a matter of definition. It depends upon how far one regards a genuine understanding of the substance of the text as still being the task of historical and critical method itself.

7. If one follows the usage which is normal among exegetes of referring only to the study of the layers of meaning within the Old Testament itself as the task of "historical criticism" then one cannot accept as permissible the limitation of the Christian interpretation of the scripture to this task alone. "It is doubtful whether it is sufficient in providing an introduction to the Bible for Christian people to accompany a translation by literary and historical notes which show how those who were originally addressed could have understood their texts. Such notes can be completely orthodox without fulfilling what is expected of them: everything is there except the essential." Over and above the establishing of the original sense of an utterance, one must erect thereupon a *further process of exegesis, which goes on to give the total statement of the scripture.* Only at this point do we enter the region where the scripture is God's word to us, and where it is therefore inerrant.

What form this process of exegesis should take is not easy to say. The scripture as a unity is a structure of so many dimensions that it is not easy to master. The last few pages may have given the impression that the utterance intended in individual biblical texts is to be found by trimming them down in the light of the scripture as a whole. As a definitive view, this would be unquestionably false. The New Testament represents not merely the crisis of the Old, but also its fulfillment. Thus in this process of the exegesis of the scripture as a whole, one must also draw on the light which Christ sheds on the Old Testament. Of the methods of the past, one may leave ingenious allegorizations to such as Paul Claudel.

True typology can be taken more seriously. It can be carried out in a way which makes clear what our present purpose must be: the exemplification of the *analogia fidei* in its historical dimensions. It is not by chance that an important group of Protestant Old Testament scholars has again been able to agree on a program for "typology." Yet such methods, which in their concrete application tend not to regard the single biblical text in its context, seem rather to belong to the realm of preaching. In academic theology, it is not possible, at least at the present moment, to attain to the sense intended by the scripture as a unity without standing back to some extent from individual texts. In practice, one will reach the inerrant sense of scripture only in biblical theology. By this we mean the theology of the Bible as a whole which can be derived from the theology of individual subjects in the Bible, and it is still not possible at the present day to name any convincing example of such a theology of the whole Bible. Perhaps, moreover, one should not try to construct such a theology as a "biblical" theology; instead, in a conscious awareness that one is also accepting the tradition, which no scriptural exegete can exclude from the understanding which he brings to the scripture, one should at once construct a dogmatic theology, but one which is drawn more fully from the Bible than is the practice today.

One so well acquainted with the problem as Henri de Lubac says of Thomas Aquinas, whose hermeneutic principle is wholly that of the spiritual sense, and in his scriptural commentaries proceeds in the traditional typological fashion, that "the spiritual interpretation which is really his own is the great doctrinal structure of his *Summa*." Perhaps in the course of time we shall see the development in theology of techniques of exegesis which are once again close to the scripture and lend to the infallible sense of scripture, but which are not wholly separated from the text like biblical or dogmatic theology, and do not turn into an extraneous system. At present, however, we do not possess such techniques. In straightforward Christian practice things are simpler. Anyone who within the worship of the New Testament community listens to the proclamation of an Old Testament text is already hearing it in the context of the encounter with Christ; and here we are not thinking of the ingenious secondary application of the scripture in the lessons chosen for the feasts of Our Lady, but of normal Old Testament texts understood in their literal sense, which it is to be hoped the coming reform of the lectionary will increase. Moreover, anyone who continues his encounter with the scripture in the liturgy through private reading and meditation on the scripture will normally read the Old Testament from the New Testament understanding which his faith brings to it.

8. To conclude: in the light of the theses we have profounded, biblical inerrancy is seen to be simply a *special aspect of the truth of divine revelation*. It ceases to be an item of theological tradition which can be associated only in an external and superficial fashion to the central event of revelation, and of which many Christians are aware only through the fact that it presents difficulties to their faith. If a new theory of biblical inspiration were to place the subject wholly in the context of the New Testament and the self-fulfillment of the primitive Church, it would probably for the most part come to the same conclusion as this study, which has proceeded from the problems of the Old Testament. Hugo of St. Victor says: *Omnis Scriptura Divina unus liber est, et ille unus liber Christus est.* ("The whole divine Scripture is one book, and this one book is Christ.")

# CHAPTER THREE

# THE STORY OF THE FALL

The story of the fall of the first man stands isolated and in the margin of the Old Testament. No other narrative, no prophetic writing, and no psalm mentions it. Only the latest wisdom writings appear to know of it — but they already assume the canon as authoritative. Thus we must conclude that the story of the fall played no part in the personal religious faith of the Israelites before the exile and in the classical worship of Israel. At that period it only existed in literature, in what is known as the Yahwist history, which after the exile in Babylon was to become one of the sources of the Pentateuch. It began not as an article of living faith, but as theological theory.

Later, however, it attained a quite different standing in religious consciousness. It came to be one of the pillars of the teaching of Paul's Epistle to the Romans. Through the Christian doctrine of original sin which was developed from it, and from the Epistle to the Romans, it came to be so central to dogmatic theology that, even at present, it is normal in some theological faculties to pass straight on, once it has been discussed, to christology — omitting all the rest of the Old Testament. It is hardly possible to give the Yahwist story of the fall a more prominent place in the consciousness of faith at the expense of other parts of the Bible. When one considers that philosophers, and especially the German idealists, repeatedly have attempted to interpret this story, one may well term it a key text for the Western interpretation of the reality of evil.

It is only natural that in the course of the astonishing history of its influence, this text repeatedly has been overlaid and encrusted with new layers of understanding and interpretation. But our modern consciousness obliges us to consider the question of its original meaning. This exegetical question is no more than preparatory to theology proper. It must be complemented in many respects before a theological statement which is relevant to the present day can be propounded. But even today, it is indispensable as a preliminary to a theology of evil. What is it, then, which biblical scholarship, inquiring in historical and critical terms into the original meaning of the text, finds in the story of the fall?

The fable which the story tells is simple. Yahweh-Elohim forms man from the earth and blows the breath of life into him. He places him in the garden, gives him a commandment, and provides a woman for him as his companion. Then the serpent tempts the woman. The woman and the man eat of the forbidden fruit. Yahweh-Elohim calls the man, the woman, and the serpent to task. Then he passes judgment upon the serpent, the woman, and the man and drives them out of the garden, so that they cannot eat from the tree of life. What, then, was the original significance of this story?

Within our present framework, we may ignore all preliminary questions of textual criticism, literary criticism and the history of the formation of the story as it stands. Nor do I wish to repeat here the familiar conclusions of earlier exegesis, such as, for example, the fact that in the dialogue between the serpent and the woman (Gen 3:1–6) a quite astounding psychology of temptation is assumed. These things are already known. Instead, I wish to develop a number of theological aspects of the story of the fall which have become evident as a result of the new possibilities and the methods now available to modern biblical study. We shall first attempt to distinguish the specific nature of the story of the fall by comparison with other ancient Eastern texts. Second, we shall consider the same story from the point of view of the *history of tradition*. Third, we shall look at the *history of its redaction*, examining the theology of the Yahwist. I trust that in this whole study it will be possible to distinguish the theology which in the biblical text is transformed by a sublime mastery of artistic devices into a pure narrative; for from the very start we must affirm that we are dealing in Genesis 2 and 3 not with archaic simplicity, but with advanced theology, which, however, is conducted not like our own, in discursive and abstract terms, but by molding figures and actions into shape.

### A Comparison With Ancient Near Eastern Texts
### (Evil as Sin)

We possess Mesopotamian parallels to the narrative of the flood in Genesis, which for practical purposes are also flood narratives. They are similar to the biblical story, not merely in individual elements, but in their general theme, the range of their material and in their whole intention. There is no such parallel to the Yahwist narrative of the primal sin of the parents of the race. Nor is it even the case that the mere chance of archaeology has so far deprived us of complete parallels, but that tomorrow or the next day may suddenly supply them in the form of new cuneiform tablets. There will probably never be an exact parellel, because the Yahwist narrative of the fall seems to have been composed much more independently than, for example, the Yahwist flood narrative.

There are nevertheless parallels to individual narrative themes of the story of the fall. The story makes full use of set themes of mythology and epic. There is a deity who kneads into shape the first man, the garden of God, the great world rivers, the plant of life, the serpent who harms man, a deity who clothes man, the guarding of sacred gates by cherubim and a zigzag sword. All of these are structural elements of mythology and epic, more or less familiar to us in the most various contexts, which were at the disposal of the Yahwist. He handles them quite freely in building up his narrative. All of these elements were by their origin and further use associated with other particular themes, with fixed conventions about how they were applied, and with particular key words and emotional contents in mythical theology. Anyone who took up any of these elements was quoting a whole realm of utterances. It was possible to quote these themes simply in order to affirm these utterances. It was also possible to quote them in order to reject or invert the statements they implied. What does the Yahwist make of the mythical and epic themes which he quotes?

In so posing the question, we have found the legitimate starting point for our comparison with ancient Near-Eastern material. We shall not assert literary dependence — all previous attempts to do this have failed. We shall merely seek to locate the means of expression which the Yahwist possessed in the appropriate context for their understanding. In the paragraphs that follow we shall restrict ourselves to two ancient set themes, the shaping of man by a deity, and the inaccessibility of the plant of life.

The fall narrative of the Yahwist begins with the forming of man from the dust of the earth: "Yahweh-Elohim formed man of dust from the ground, and breathed into his nostrils the breath of life" (Gen 2:7). Now there is no question that chapters 2 and 3 of Genesis are dealing with the fall, with the origin of suffering and death, and not with the creation of man. The frequently repeated term "the second creation narrative" is fundamentally false. Genesis 2 is not an independent narrative, but the exposition leading to the story of the fall. Thus one ought to ask why this exposition goes back to the creation of man. Was it necessary to give an explicit account here of the forming of man from the earth? It was in fact necessary, as will be seen when we compare it with a mythological text.

This text is the sixth table of the cosmogonic poem *Enuma Elish*, which was recited in full by a priest of the cultic idol of Bel in Babylon on the fourth day of the New Year feast. The sixth table describes in lines 1–38 how the creation of men came about. Men were created by being formed from the blood of the god Kingu, who was killed for this purpose, or according to a variant from the flesh and blood of the god, mixed with clay. What is common to the biblical text and *Enuma Elish* is the theme of the forming of man from a material already available. But we now turn to the mythological context of the theme. There is guilt among the gods. Apsu and Mummu have been killed, and thereby death has come into being. Kingu, the leader of the divine rebels, is chained. The assembly of the gods condemns him to serve as the means of taking evil away again from the realm of the gods. To this end he is killed, and mankind is created from his blood. Thus the guilt which had come into being in the divine realm is enclosed and eternalized in the mortal existence of man, prey to all kind of evil. At the same time, the gods themselves are freed from it. It is this, at least according to the interpretation given to this text by R. Labat, which is the service which man has to carry out for the gods. Men serve the gods through the cult. But as a preliminary to this, they already serve the gods through their very existence — since they are basically nothing more than the evil rejected from the divine realm, which thereby becomes pure and holy again. The consequences of this mythological statement for a theology of evil are clear. Evil is involved in the very existence of man. It has come to him from the divine realm itself. The meaning of human existence lies in the inclusion of evil in his life.

If one assumes that such bodies of assertions, linked with the theme of the forming of man, were current in the ancient Near East, then it is evidently of significance that the Yahwist does not describe man as being formed from the blood of gods, impregnated with guilt, but simply from the dust of the earth. The shaping of man from the earth becomes a kind of opposing thesis — or one might even call it a "demythologizing." The Yahwist sees evil as coming into creation in a different way from the myth. It does not come until after man has been created. It is not involved in his existence, but comes from his freedom. Evil derives from human sin.

We turn now to the second comparison which we wish to make, that concerning the plant of life. In the Yahwist it appears as the "tree of life" which stands in the Garden of God, beside the "tree of knowledge of good and evil." After their sin men are excluded by Yahweh-Elohim from the garden, so that they may not eat of the tree of life and thereby attain to eternal life (Gen 3:22 f.). Thus we do not have here the simple theme of the "plant of life," but the more complex theme of the "inaccessibility of the plant of life." This states, in a pictorial convention, that man must die. How does it come about that man is not to succeed in eating the plant of life?

The Gilgamesh epic, the *Iliad* or *Beowulf* of the ancient Near East, gives an answer to this decisive question in its concluding scene, at the end of table 11. The problem of life occupies a large part of the Gilgamesh epic. After the death of his friend Enkidu, Gilgamesh wanders from land to land: "If I die, will I not then be like Enkidu? Sorrow has seized my entrails. Fearing death, I roam across the plains." He is seeking immortality. As he journeys, the goddess who gives gifts calls to him: "Gilgamesh, why are you hurrying from place to place? You will not find the life you seek. When the gods created men, they destined death for men. They kept life for themselves." But Gilgamesh does not listen. And at the very end of his wanderings, he succeeds in diving down to the bottom of the ocean and plucking the herb of life there. Its thorns prick his hands, but he holds it firm and comes to the surface with it. Instead of eating it at once, he, the king of Uruk, resolves to carry it to his city, so that his whole people may become young again with him. On his way home, he has to go across vast deserts, and when he arrives, hot and dusty, at a spring, which invites him to bathe in it, he jumps into the cool water. Then the serpent smells the scent of the herb of life, comes, eats the herb and departs. Gilgamesh sees how the fleeing serpent sheds its skin. The herb of life has already worked, and made it young again. But Gilgamesh has been cheated out of the herb. He stands and utters a cry of despair. After all his wanderings, he has to return empty-handed to Uruk.

In the Bible the plant of life is also forbidden to man, once again through the intervention of the serpent. But here too we find an antithesis to the myth. In the Gilgamesh epic the loss of the plant of life is due to chance and fate, or perhaps even to the wholly irrational will of the gods. According to the Yahwist, what happens is determined by an act of man's freedom. Access to the tree of life is forbidden because of sin. The serpent can only appear as the tempter, and no longer as the thief of life. Man is robbed because of what he does himself.

The two comparisons which we have carried out show not

only the mythological source from which the Yahwist has derived individual structural elements of his narrative, and not only the technique with which he demythologizes and reinterprets them, but also lead us to the central statement by which everything previously implicit in the themes adopted is transformed in the Yahwist narrative: the evil in the world comes from human freedom, which is realized as sin.

But how does the Yahwist come to derive what is evil and dark in creation from human freedom? And which are the hidden forces which determine the structure of his narrative, ever in detail? These are questions which can no longer be answered by a comparison with the ancient Near East, but lead us instead to the traditions of Israel.

### *An Interpretation in the Light of the History of Tradition*
### *(Sin as a Breach of the Covenant)*

The worship and theology of Israel were formed more than anything else by the idea of the covenant with God. Yahweh had concluded a covenant, that is, a treaty with Israel. The election of Israel from among all other nations took concrete form in the covenant. As God's covenant people, Israel began its march toward the future.

Recent scholarship has brought about important new insights into the structure of the concept of the covenant. These have shown that Israel's treaty with God was understood on the analogy of the vassallage treaties, by which small kingdoms associated themselves with one of the emperors in the great international system of the late Bronze Age in the ancient Near East. It is not possible here to go into detail. But at least we are able today to give a fairly accurate account of the conceptions, processes of thought and even forms of words in Israel which were typical of the covenant tradition, and distinguished it from other Israelite traditions.

The covenant tradition was kept alive through the covenant worship. Through this worship, it was also a present reality to every Israelite. Moreover, even in texts where this was not at first suspected, such as the prophets and many of the psalms, exegesis has discovered references to the covenant tradition.

It is an astonishing fact that the Yahwist's narrative of the fall in Genesis 2 and 3 is determined in a concealed way by the covenant tradition. It is so astonishing, for the Yahwist too sees the covenant with God as the exclusive property of the people of Israel. It first appeared in history at Sinai, after it already had been anticipated in the covenant with Abraham. For this reason, the word "covenant" naturally does not appear in Genesis 2 and 3. Nor is it the Yahwist's intention in any way to say that a "covenant" existed between the "man" of Genesis 2 and 3, and Yahweh-Elohim. But the form which the narrative now takes in Genesis 2 and 3 would not have been possible without the covenant theology of Israel. It is from this that the Yahwist knows that evil is the fruit of sin. It is from the covenant that he can define sin as the transgression of a commandment of God. It is also from the covenant that he comes to know of human freedom which rebels against God.

The link between the covenant tradition and Genesis 2 and 3 can also be demonstrated on the level of vocabulary, but in the framework of the present discussion we shall content ourselves with a comparison between the course of the narrative of the fall and the typical series of statements which summarizes the theology of the covenant. In what context does the covenant theology see the sin of Israel? Roughly speaking, the following series of successive statements occur. First, Yahweh found, created, and chose Israel outside the land of Canaan, in Egypt or in the wilderness. Second, Yahweh graciously led Israel into the wonderful land of Canaan, to dwell there. Third, Yahweh imposed the commandments upon Israel as the conditions of his covenant. Fourth, if the people of Israel observe the commandments of Yahweh, all will go well with them, in the country into which Yahweh has led them. As the covenant worship briefly formulates it, Israel will "live." Fifth, if Israel does not observe the commandments of Yahweh, then Yahweh will bring into operation the curses associated with the covenant. Israel will be visited by plagues, driven out of its land by enemies and led into exile, and finally will be destroyed. The covenant cult briefly sums up all of this by saying that Israel will "die." This series of statements was in the first instance an ideal pattern of history. But this pattern, as the Deuteronomic history attempts to show, was then realized in its entirety in the history of Israel. In this series of statements the sin of Israel appears as the transgression of commandments. It is a breach of the covenant. Every evil which comes upon Israel is the consequence of the breach of the covenant. By contrast, from faithfulness to the covenant comes the ability to live in the land, that is, within the sphere of blessing.

This series of assertions in the covenant theology is also the key to the course of the Yahwist narrative of the fall. In Genesis 2 and 3 man is first created in the wilderness, outside the garden. Second, Yahweh-Elohim places man in the wonderful garden. Third, Yahweh-Elohim gives him a commandment, the observance of which is the condition for the fourth point, that he should "live" in the garden (for the "tree of life" stands in the garden). But fifth, man transgresses the commandment and must consequently "die," that is, he comes under the curse and must leave the garden.

This correspondence is not fortuitous. Rather, it shows that the set themes of myth and epic which were available for a description of the origin of the world and mankind were polarized by a mode of thought which derived from the covenant tradition. The concrete form taken by the existing narrative of the fall would have been impossible before Israel's fundamental experience of revelation. It represents a reflection upon the entry of evil into the world at the beginning of history, on the basis of a religious experience which was first given and thought out within Israel's covenant with God. It is only through the idea of the covenant that all the dark side of human existence came to be regarded as a consequence of sin, and sin as an act of human freedom. If Israel had not thought of its relationship with God in the explicitly juridical categories of a treaty, then it would not have been as conscious of the element of freedom in sin, and of the connection between sin and evildoing.

On the other hand, in our theological interpretation of the narrative of the fall, we must take account of the known traditional background. The emphasis lies upon the free act of Adam. The serpent who is the tempter is by contrast really no more than a piece of mythological stage furniture which has already been demythologized. The whole narrative setting of the act of sin is to be thought of in the first instance simply as a means for making the statement concerning the freely committed sin possible. The justification for turning individual statements in this whole complex of assertions into independent theological theses would have to be argued separately.

However, the demonstration of the formative influence of the covenant tradition on the Yahwist's doctrine of sin explains only one thing: the categories in which he thinks about the sin of the parents of the race. This provides no answer to the quite different question which must finally be asked. Of whom is the Yahwist actually speaking? Who is Adam, "the man"? Does the Yahwist really think of him as the "first man," that is, is the thought here historical? Or is he a mythological "primal man," that is, a symbol for all men, for each individual and for all together?

The answer to this new question may perhaps be given step by step. In the first place, the typical device used in the myth of the beginning of time — that of concentrating in the primal and original figure what is valid for all times and places — is by no means completely excluded from the material of these two chapters. The typological connection with the theology of Israel's covenant in fact still demands this approach. Every human sin and its consequences are described in the sin of Adam. This fact should not be denied. Even the apostle Paul seems to have taken the text in this sense in Romans 7.

But at the same time one must also go a step further. There is present at the same time the intention of making a genuine historical statement. Naturally it would be meaningless to speak of an "historical" text. The text derives from human reflection, not from the manipulation of documents and records. The German language describes the latter activity of the human mind, and the kind of knowledge which derives from it, by the word *Historie*, which is limited in its application to this aspect of history. The word of much wider application which is appropriate here is *Geschichte*, although in this context the word ought not to be isolated, in the manner of existentialist philosophy, from the objective time to which it refers.

The realm of history in the sense of the word *Geschichte* is not merely the object of scientific historical activity, but also that of human reflection. A philosophy of history and a theology of history arise from human reflection upon history. Both are equally concerned, albeit in a wholly different sense from factual history in the sense of the German word *Historie*, with the factual events of the past. It is our thesis that the Yahwist's narrative of the fall is intended to be a genuine historical statement, in the sense of *Geschichte*, reflective and interpretative history, but not of *Historie*, factual and scientific history. Our task is to define this intention more precisely. It can only be elucidated from the whole context of the Yahwist work, the opening scene of which is found in Genesis 2 and 3.

### The History of the Redaction of the Yahwist Work (or the History of Doom and Salvation)

The Yahwist work, which as we now find it is combined in the Pentateuch with the Elohist work and the so-called priestly writing to form a single historical narrative, leads the reader first of all from the parents of the race, through the early history of man, to Abraham. To this extent, it surveys all the nations of the world. But from Abraham on, its horizon is limited to his descendants. The narrative continues through the patriarchal period, through the servitude in Egypt, the liberation from Egypt, and the period in the wilderness, as far as the borders of the Promised Land. It is possible that an account of the entry and occupation of Canaan was also included, but this is disputed by scholars.

The Yahwist worked by collecting and combining the individual traditions of his people which were available in oral or perhaps already in written form. This does not mean that he may not have incorporated statements of his own into the whole work. At best, the Yahwist can claim only the character of strict historical writing for individual parts of his work. In other parts, the material available to him did not permit this. But everywhere he presents, along with the material that is available to him, a theology of history. How does he express this? First, by the order in which he presents the material, by the choice and the order of his narratives — but also, at decisive points, by texts formulated in his own words. There is no doubt that he himself carefully worded the narrative of Genesis 2 and 3, precisely because it is the opening narrative of the whole work. But there are also other key texts. The study of this redactional process must seek to isolate the writer's key texts by exact analysis of his redactional work, and to deduce from them what it is that he wishes to assert.

In what follows, we shall restrict ourselves to the most important key text of the Yahwist work, which occurs at the very point at which it passes from the early history of man to the history of the patriarchs, that is, where the horizon of the narrative is first restricted to the people of Israel. There the Yahwist, in words of his own, presents Yahweh as saying to Abram: "Go from your country and your kindred and your father's house to the land that I will show you. And I will make of you a great nation, and I will bless you, and make your name great, so that you will be a blessing. I will bless those who bless you, and him who curses you I will curse; and in you all the families of the earth shall be blessed" (Gen 12:1-3).

The key word in this text is "bless." Thus the meaning of the history of the people of Israel which begins with Abraham is the coming of blessing into the world. The text here reveals the meaning of the preceding history of the early days of mankind — man had lacked this one thing: "blessing." The word "bless" has not previously occurred, but the word "curse" has. The curse came into being with the first sin, the curse increased with Cain, the flood was the further effect of the curse, and so forth. The curse extends over the entire realm of the nations — and then Yahweh sets up in Abraham and his descendants a separate enclave of blessing. But this blessing — and this is the highest point of the Yahwist's theology of history — exists in Israel, but not for Israel alone. The blessing is to overflow — in a future which is still unknown to the Yahwist himself — over all the families of the earth.

Thus what we said above is shown to be false, that with Abraham the horizon of the Yahwist became limited to Israel. This is not the case. Even though the historical narrative is now restricted to Israel, this history is recounted only because it is to be of importance for all the families of the earth.

Thus the scope of the Yahwist's theology of history is universal. It is only because Israel is intended to become a blessing for all nations that the Yahwist constructed a universal history of the origins of all mankind, to precede his history of Israel. In this he is unquestionably an innovator — Israel's confession of faith, which he followed in constructing his history, began only with the patriarchs, and even the Elohist began his historical work with Abraham. The Yahwist shares the new feeling for history of the age of David and Solomon, when Israel suddenly became an empire, incorporated other nations into itself, and entered into contact and exchanged ideas with yet other nations. It was no longer possible to make the naïve claim that Yahweh's election was for his own people alone. The question arose: what about other nations? Why did Yahweh choose us, although the whole earth belongs to him? The answer which the Yahwist finds to this question is that of the universal blessing of the nations, which is to be the conclusion of the history of the people of Israel. Why this blessing can be reintroduced only gradually into the realm of history is shown by the preceding history of the early days of mankind, which is the history of a universal curse, spreading as mankind does.

We do not need to examine the Yahwist's theology of history in greater detail. It is sufficient to be aware of the universal scale on which it is planned. The Yahwist is concerned with all nations and all ages. The universal horizon is essential to this theology. It also decisively affects the purpose and intention of the first narrative in this work, the story of the sin of the parents of the race. This narrative deals with the beginning of the universal history of mankind. Wherever or whenever this beginning may have taken place, and whatever concrete form it may have possessed (for the narrative itself makes use of the set themes of mythology and a covenant theology read back into the past), the intention of the narrative is in any case to assert that at the very beginning of the whole history of mankind sin came into the world, and with it its consequences: the placing of mankind in the realm where the curse of death prevails. Paul rightly understood this narrative in Romans 5. And although the way the first sin is recounted is such that it must also be described as the original type of every human sin, it nevertheless implies an act of freedom at the beginning. This is the answer to the question posed by this third part of our study. The narrative of the first sin is also historical in its intention.

## Final Considerations

We may perhaps sum up the results we have obtained by introducing the idea of theodicy. The question of the "justification of God" is posed by the Yahwist in a very original way. The Yahwist's faith is that of Israel, and he is therefore convinced that God has chosen his people and preserves them from every evil. From this point of view he has no problem of theodicy. But as a man who lived in the age of David and Solomon, he has now experienced an immense widening of his field of vision. Israel suddenly becomes an empire. Other nations come within the scope of his actual experience. They are not blessed by Yahweh like Israel. How is this possible? Why do other nations of the world come under the darkness of the curse? For the Yahwist, the problem of theodicy takes the form of this question, posed to the Lord of history.

His answer is twofold. He states first that the darkness over the nations does not come from God — as Mesopotamian mythology asserted — but from man. The first men sinned, and their sin was constantly repeated. The basis of the curse which lies upon the nations is this constantly rising tide of free human choices of evil. God may not be accused on this account. In fact, from the very first, God is at work to bring his blessing back into a world which is giving itself over to the curse. This is the beginning of a type of theodicy which we may call the "demonstration of the opposite": "God is not guilty, but man" — this is the first form of theodicy, the "demonstration of the innocence of God." The "demonstration of the opposite" shows that God is not merely innocent of the darkness of creation, but that he is in fact constantly at work to bring light back into it. This again is a technique of theodicy which is also used by the Odyssey. There the assembly of the gods at the beginning makes it clear that the whole epic of the return of Odysseus is intended to demonstrate one thing alone: that Zeus does not allow an excess of suffering to fall upon an innocent man, but finally transforms the suffering he has undergone in his wanderings into the happiness of his return home.

In the same way the Yahwist in his theodicy makes the experience of Israel the starting point of a "demonstration of the opposite." Since the time of Abraham God has been at work bringing light into the darkness of the world of the nations: by the blessing upon Abraham and his descendants. Because the whole world of the nations lies in the darkness of the curse, the blessing upon Israel will be only the beginning of God's blessing. Israel is only the bridgehead from which Yahweh's blessing will go out to conquer the whole creation. At the end of the ages — which for the Yahwist, too, still lay in the future — the word which the Yahwist makes God utter as a promise to Abraham will be fulfilled. Let us quote it once again, in the form in which Paul takes it up in Galatians 3:8: "In you shall all the nations be blessed."

Only because the Yahwist knew that he could introduce this statement at the beginning of the history of Abraham could he dare to describe so consistently, in his history of the early days of mankind, the mighty curse which lies upon the whole of mankind and upon all ages. The narrative of the fall in Genesis is not a theodicy merely because it pronounces God innocent of all evil, and accuses the freedom of sinful man of responsibility for all the darkness of history. It is a theodicy far more because that only represents the dark side of God's action in blessing, which in conflict with sin and the suffering which comes from it, will ultimately be extended to all the nations of the earth through Abraham and his seed. But the seed of Abraham — Paul goes on to say — is Christ.

# CHAPTER FOUR

# THE SONG OF VICTORY AT THE RED SEA

## Exodus 15:1–18

Our liturgy is constructed above all from biblical texts. In it the Bible, and above all the Old Testament, is often used not in its original sense, but according to the laws of metaphorical correspondence, symbolic association, ingenious allusion or allegorical application, or, in short, of typology.

### Liturgical Typology

A few texts from the very rich mass for the feast of Corpus Christi may serve as an introduction to the world of thought in which this intellectual game is played. This mass was composed at the climax of the Middle Ages, and it is highly probable that its material was composed by Thomas Aquinas. What is done without reflection in old liturgical texts is worked out here according to a very conscious theory. Thus in the hymn *Lauda Sion* we find the following stanza concerning the eucharist:

> In figures it is anticipated:
> When Isaac is sacrificed,
> and the Paschal Lamb is instituted,
> when the fathers receive the manna.

> *In figuris praesignatur*
> *cum Isaac immolatur*
> *agnus Paschae deputatur*
> *datur manna patribus.*

67

Thus the long line of figurative correspondence extends from the Old Testament to the New. The two realities are parallel, and can even interpenetrate each other. One can draw its name from the other — as it is done in another stanza of the *Lauda Sion*:

> At this table of the new king
> the new Pasch of the new law
> ends the old Passover.

> *In hac mensa novi regis*
> *novum Pascha novae legis*
> *Phase vetus terminat.*

Thus there is a new king, a new Passover and a new law. Here, however, the movement of all biblical and liturgical typology is always in one direction: from the former shadow to the new reality.

Those who created our liturgies saw their great task in repeatedly following this path. The mysteries of the new covenant set forth and contained in our liturgy are repeatedly expressed in terms of the ancient types of the Old Testament, through rites, psalms, lessons and interpretative texts. Great skill in perceiving the concordance between the two Testaments was required of everyone who desired to take part in the liturgy with understanding. Thomas Aquinas interrupts his hymn on the sacrament of the altar to marvel for a whole stanza simply upon the miracle of the passage from one Testament to the other:

> Newness drives out the old,
> reality the shadow,
> light does away with night.

> *Vetustatem novitas*
> *umbram fugat veritas*
> *noctem lux eliminat.*

This is the basic rule of this way of handling scripture: once the correspondence between the two Testaments has been found, the next stage is the surpassing of the Old Testament by the New. This correspondence and opposition combined to form the spiritual dialectic of the two Testaments. The creative period of our liturgy experienced the fruitfulness of the scripture by acquiescing completely in this dialectic between the Testaments. It saturated the liturgy with it, clothing its spiritual experience and its religious utterance in this intellectual game of images.

Thus typology is firmly rooted in our liturgical heritage. It forms its basic structure. The liturgy constantly calls to us to accept it. If we refuse to think, experience, and pray in typological terms, we run the risk of remaining strangers, who are never at home in the liturgy. Moreover, every liturgical reform must face the question, whether or not it affirms the basic pattern of this ancient structure.

### Typology as a Problem

But can we nowadays honestly think in typological terms? Does it not become a superficial game? Have we not here a conflict between the modern and the ancient consciousness, between historical thought and symbolical and speculative thought? In fact, is not the true meaning of holy scripture, which modern exegesis is able to elucidate more exactly than any previous age, in conflict with these elegant but inexact games played by an earlier age? Should we not nowadays try to create for ourselves a new liturgy which abandons the typological game and uses biblical texts only in their literal sense?

The question is rarely uttered in such radical terms. But it lies behind more proposals for reform than many would like to think. It is a serious question, perhaps the most serious in the whole question of the reform of the liturgy. For it touches its basic structure. The study that follows does not attempt to give any fundamental answer, but to examine in the light of the question that has been posed a single biblical text, which, however, belongs to the very heart of liturgical typology.

### The Typology of the Paschal Night and Modern Exegesis

Among the readings in the celebration of the Easter Vigil which remain even after it has been shortened, occurs the account of the passage of the children of Israel through the Sea in Exodus 14. The canticle which follows it is the next passage in the biblical text, Moses' song of victory, although at the present day only the opening verses are sung. According to ancient accounts of our liturgy, it was originally sung in its entirety. The study which follows takes as its subject this song of victory.

The collect which follows sets out its application to the baptism which in fact follows in the liturgy of the Easter Vigil:

> "What your mighty arm did to one people, when you saved them from the Egyptian pursuers, you carry out for the salvation of the (many) Gentiles by the water of rebirth; therefore vouchsafe that the whole world may be lifted up to be children of Abraham, and to the dignity of Israel."

At an earlier point in the Easter Vigil liturgy the identity of the nights already has been proclaimed in the *Exultet*. The night "in which once you led our fathers, the children of Israel, out of Egypt and guided them dry shod through the Red Sea," the night "in which Christ broke the bonds of death and rose victoriously from the grave," and the present night in which in the baptism of new Christians "vices are driven out, sins washed away," and in which those who repent are reconciled ("to those who have fallen it gives back innocence, to those who mourn, joy") — all these nights are one and the same "truly blessed night, which spoiled the Egyptians, enriched the Hebrews, joined heaven with earth and God with man." The gap in time no longer exists, the types coalesce, and the unity of the divine work of salvation is present in the act of worship. The Fathers of the Church never tire of expounding this typological interpretation of the passage through the Red Sea, the theologians of the Middle Ages took it up in their turn, and it is only modern exegesis which is no longer prepared to do this.

Modern exegesis places the Old Testament text in its original historical context, attempts to understand it in that setting with the minimum of falsification, and no longer finds any link which connects it with traditional typology.

From the point of view of the liturgy this is a decline from a level previously attained. Should one despise modern exegesis or — more modestly — at least ignore it and reject its help?

I think not. For modern exegesis is in accordance with the consciousness we now possess. With its prudence and care, and even in its cautiousness and reticence, it is the only way in which our own abilities and longings can be expressed, not in ingenious procedures which perhaps satisfied the feeling of an earlier age, but which would no longer be honest. Thus one must take the protests of the exegetes seriously. If it were not possible to return, on the basis of modern exegesis and through its own means, to something approaching liturgical typology, then we would have to abandon this typology.

The deep concern of modern exegesis is for the literal sense. Thus we must formulate our requirement as follows: If it cannot be shown that the biblical text concerning the passage through the Red Sea is already typological in its purpose, then we shall have to abandon its typological use at the present day, and the reading of Exodus 14, and also the *Exsultet*, would have to disappear from our Easter Vigil.

This requirement seems a severe one. I have insisted upon it, in the first place, because it must be insisted upon at the present day, and second, because I believe that in fact it can be satisfied. So long as we do not pose such a severe requirement, we are dishonest. We would be behaving as though nothing had changed and as though we could set aside our modern consciousness in worship, and forget scientific scholarship. But we would perhaps be depriving ourselves of the possibility of so conducting our scientific study that in certain circumstances it could find a place, through its own methods and approach, for what was obvious to tradition, and which is perhaps only apparently in conflict with modern exegesis. In my view, the latter is possible in the case of Moses' song of victory.

I do not suggest that because it is possible here, it is possible on principle throughout the Old Testament. We must guard at the present day against any generalization in exegesis which is not carefully substantiated. We must attempt to understand the distinctive nature of each separate case, drawing the appropriate consequences from it. We are examining now only Exodus 15, Moses' song of victory, to see whether it may be possible, by consistently carrying out an exegesis on modern lines, to come to terms with the traditional typological interpretation.

## The Text of Exodus 15:1–19

The song of Moses is one of the oldest texts of the Bible. Orthographical peculiarities in the original Hebrew text show that it was not only in existence, but already had been written down by the period of the Judges, that is, shortly after the entry of the Israelites into Palestine. Later changes in the meaning of words, alterations in standard spelling, interpretative interpolations and the like have produced a somewhat difficult text, out of which it is possible to produce a translation which is in agreement with the original text only by the use of textual criticism and detailed philological study. In fact, in the past twenty years much work of this kind has been carried out on Exodus 15.

The result has been to make it increasingly clear that the song is a hymn, which was probably sung regularly in the worship of Israel — and we may assume that this was at the Passover festival. After an introduction (v. 1) and a brief praise of God in the first person, which is probably a later literary interpolation (v. 2), the song proper begins, and it possesses a very regular structure. One can think of it as being rendered by two choirs, one of which sang of the power of God, while the other alternated with it and narrated God's historical act of salvation. We may distinguish the two choirs as the "praising" and the "narrative" choirs. The layout of the translation which follows displays the structure of the song.

(1) Then Moses and the Israelites sang this song for Yahweh:

I will sing to Yahweh,
  for he is highly exalted.
Horse and chariot
  he has thrown into the sea.

(2) My strength and my protection is Yahweh,
  and he has become my salvation.
This is my God — and I will praise him!
My father's God — I will exalt him!

(3) Yahweh is a hero of war,
  Yahweh is his name.

(4)  Pharaoh's chariots he cast into the sea,
     sank into the Sea of Reeds his best warriors.

(5)  The floods covered them,
     they went into the depths like a stone.

(6)  Thy right hand, Yahweh,
     O terrible and mighty,
thy right hand, Yahweh,
     shatters the enemy.

(7)  In the fullness of thy majesty
     thou destroyest thine adversaries.
Thou sendest forth thy fury,
     it consumes them like stubble.

(8)  At the blast of thy nostrils
     the waters piled up.
The waves stood up like a wall,
     the floods congealed in the midst of the sea.

(9)  The enemy said,
     "I will pursue, I will overtake,
I will divide the spoil,
     the throat will be satisfied,
I will draw my sword,
     my hand seizes it."

(10)  Thou didst blow with thy breath,
     the sea covered them.
They sank as lead
     in the terrible waters.

(11)  Who is like thee
     Among the gods, Yahweh?
Who is like thee,
     terrible among the holy ones?
Fearful in deeds,
     doing wonders?

(12)  Thou didst stretch out thy right hand,
     the underworld swallowed them.

(13)  Thou didst lead in thy steadfast love
     the people whom thou hast redeemed.
Thou didst guide them in thy strength
     on to thy holy pasture.

(14) The people heard it —
    they trembled.
    Trembling seized
    the princes of the Philistines.

(15) Now are dismayed
    the bulls of Edom.
    The rams of Moab
    fear seized.
    They shudder,
    all the princes of Canaan.

(16) Thou castest over them
    Terror and dread.
    Before the power of thine arm
    they grew as still as stone —
    During the passing by
    of thy people, Yahweh,
    during the passing by
    of the people whom thou hast purchased.

(17) Thou hast brought them in and planted them
    on the mountain which is thine own.
    A dais for thy throne
    hast thou created, Yahweh.
    A sanctuary, my Lord,
    have thy hands established.

(18) Yahweh is king
    for ever and ever.

(19) When the horses of Pharaoh with his chariots and
his horsemen went into the sea and Yahweh brought
back the waters of the sea upon them, the people of
Israel had walked on dry ground through the midst
of the sea.

### A Detailed Exposition

The archaic character of the hymn is unmistakable. Not only
are the language, imagery and poetic form different from what we
use and value at the present day, but they also seem strange and
archaic to those who are familiar with the normal and classic texts
of the Old Testament — for the latter are several centuries more
recent. Let us first attempt to acquaint ourselves with the archaic

linguistic background of the song, in order to overcome its strangeness in this respect. For only when its unfamiliarity no longer provides an obstacle can we turn to the question which properly concerns us.

The song, according to the introduction, is for Yahweh:

> I will sing to Yahweh,
> for he is highly exalted.

The ancient Israelite divine name occurs repeatedly, ten times in all. At that time, the awe which prevented later Judaism from naming the Eternal — blessed be he — and speaking to him in a hymn informally, without a title, and without special forms of address, was unknown. Although it is the intention of this song to set forth the greatness of God, which transcends everything, he is nevertheless also Yahweh, to whom every Israelite has direct access.

> Horse and chariot
> he has thrown into the sea.

The military setting is that of the end of the Bronze Age. There were still no mounted troops. The nucleus of the army was formed by the war chariots. They were drawn by three horses, and their crew consisted of a driver and a warrior who fought on his own.

War is one of the direct human realities. Here it does not have the fearful dimensions which it possesses at the present day, nor the technical inhumanity. There is still no thought of the possibility of the fundamentally immoral character of war. Moreover, it was surrounded at that time by many rules and guarantees in international law. The decision was not easily taken to begin an unjust war — because then one could be sure of finding all one's neighbors on the side of the enemy. But when one waged a war which one was convinced was just, then it was believed possible and necessary to wage it with the help of God. And if one was victorious, perhaps even without great exertion on one's own part, then one was convinced that God had intervened. Thus for the minds of that age, war could be a genuine religious experience. This is not an experience which it is now possible for us to share. But we need not be afraid of respecting this element in our text, when it records with astonishment this new experience:

> Yahweh is a hero of war,
> Yahweh is his name.

In the narrative which follows, and which takes the form of a hymn, Yahweh himself is seen as acting. This mode of thought is not afraid of anthropomorphism, however aware it may also be of the transcendence of Yahweh.

> Pharoah's chariots he cast into the sea,
> sank into the Sea of Reeds his best warriors.
> The floods covered them,
> they went down into the depths like a stone.

What an image this is! It is an image of a God who personally casts his enemies into the sea. He takes them and throws them into the water. Let us take care not to introduce our usual conception of what took place at the "Red Sea." The god stands there, seizes his enemies and throws them into the sea. This is the image, and there is nothing more.

The words sung by the "praising" choir at once introduce a second and a third image: those of a god who raises a club to strike, and of a god who breathes fire.

> Thy right hand, Yahweh,
> O terrible and mighty,
> Thy right hand, Yahweh,
> shatters the enemy.
> In the fullness of thy majesty
> thou destroyest thine adversaries.
> Thou sendest forth thy fury,
> it consumes them like stubble.

The first image is familiar to us from the pictorial art of the ancient Near East: it is that of the deity whose right hand is raised aloft with a club in it, in order to shatter an enemy — often the chaos monster, and often human enemies.

The second image, that of a fiery breath streaming from the nose, is now taken up by the narrative choir. This breath becomes

the wind which blows over the Sea of Reeds and makes the water
back up, so that a dry path appears:

> At the blast of thy nostrils
>   the waters piled up,
> the waves stood up like a wall,
>   the floods congealed in the midst of the sea.

This image is now abandoned. The perspective changes. A
purely verbal description of what is taking place in the enemy
camp is interpolated. It describes the covetous resolve to pursue
the Israelites along the path between the waters, uttered in brief,
clipped, staccato phrases:

> The enemy said,
>   "I will pursue, I will overtake,
> I will divide the spoil,
>   the throat will be satisfied,
> I will draw my sword,
>   my hand seizes it."

At the end of the passage comes the gesture of the enemy hand
reaching out to strike. It becomes a comprehensive token for the
enemy, while there is now an immediate return to the former
wider perspective. Once again, the deity blows his breath over
the sea.

> Thou didst blow with thy breath,
>   the sea covered them.
> They sank as lead
>   in the terrible waters.

Water no longer signifies here merely the real sea, but becomes
the mythical symbol of the underworld, of death, of chaos, and
of nothingness.

Here the narrative choir has described in a powerful image
the historical act of Yahweh (there is no interest whatsoever in
the concrete historical circumstances of this act). Now the praising choir begins once again with a series of rhetorical questions
expressing praise:

> Who is like thee
>   among the gods, Yahweh?

> Who is like thee,
>     terrible among the holy ones?
> Fearful in deeds,
>     doing wonders?

Thus Yahweh is compared with the other "gods." It is not possible for us to tell with certainty whether Israel still believes here in the existence of other gods, so that a genuine comparison is intended, or whether this is merely a poetic affectation using an older mythology, like references to the Greek Olympus in the German classical poets. I would judge that the passage reflects a genuine conviction of the existence of other gods. For the Israelites, however, they are beings whom Yahweh has created and who are placed under him. They are our "angels" — though through almost the entire period of the Old Testament they are given different names: gods, sons of God, holy ones. Thus the "holy ones" of our present text refer to the "gods." It is in his great historical acts that Yahweh is manifested to Israel as one who is not on the same level as the other gods, but is the only one who is God in the full sense, since he far transcends them in terror. For Rilke, and assuredly for ancient Israel as well, even the angels are "terrible." This ancient concept, which contains a profundity of religious experiences, applies even to them. But it applies to Yahweh with a quite different intensity; it is absolutely true of him.

The narrative choir intervenes once again. After terror comes grace. A link with the preceding narrative is given first, in the image of the outstretched right hand of God:

> Thou didst stretch out thy right hand,
>     the underworld swallowed them.

The image is one of manifest revenge upon the threatening hand of the enemy. But it is followed, in a liberating contrast, by images from the nomadic and pastoral world, which for Israel in its earliest days, when it had just passed from semi-nomad life into permanent settlements, still represented the essence of everything that was good and wholesome. Yahweh is the good shepherd, who leads his people like a flock:

> Thou didst lead in thy steadfast love
>     the people whom thou hast redeemed.

Thou didst guide them in thy strength
on to thy holy pasture.

The concept of redemption comes from the law of the ancient
Near East. For a man who had been consigned to slavery, his
"redeemer" was the relation who had the duty of buying him back
on behalf of his extended family, thereby restoring to him his
freedom. Yahweh was Israel's "redeemer" from slavery in Egypt.
Yahweh purchased Israel for himself — as verse 16 states later.

Thus images of war are replaced by images of peace. But the
might of Yahweh is recounted once again. The entry of Israel
into the promised land is described as a great procession. All the
nations among whom Israel has to pass are seized by the terror
of Yahweh, stand petrified with fear, and cannot prevent the
people of God passing through their midst into the land which
is destined for them.

The people heard it —
they trembled,
Trembling seized
the prince of the Philistines.
Now are dismayed
the bulls of Edom.
The rams of Moab
fear seized.
They shudder,
all the princes of Canaan.
Thou castest over them
terror and dread.
Before the power of thine arm
they grew as still as stone —
During the passing by
of thy people, Yahweh,
During the passing by
of the people whom thou hast purchased.

The presence of these people is symbolized by their kings and
princes, and some of these are designated as the heads of their
people by the use of ancient animal names: the bulls and rams of
their people. This is once again the imagery of flocks and herds,
but the other flocks are struck still when the great and good
shepherd passes by with his flocks. They stand alongside the pro-

cessional route of Israel like stone sphinxes, and are no more than witnesses to the might of the God of Israel.

God leads Israel into his own property, into the mountain. Here ancient themes of Canaanite mythology are taken up and transferred to Yahweh. The gods dwelt upon the mountain of the gods, which was the world mountain. It was their property. It was the dais on which their throne was set up. About this throne the palace was built, the sanctuary. This whole mythological setting is now historicized and given a fixed geographical location. Yahweh, the lord of heaven and of the whole earth, has chosen Israel as his peculiar people. The whole of the land into which he is leading the people who are his own he makes his holy mountain. Israel's existence in its land is an existence lived directly in the divine realm. Even where it is secular, it is still cultic. The leading of Israel into the realm of the holy was the true purpose of the saving act of Yahweh, which is expressed in the conclusion of the narrative hymn:

> Thou hast brought them in and planted them
>   on the mountain which is thine own.
> A dais for thy throne
>   hast thou created, Yahweh.
> A sanctuary, my Lord,
>   have thy hands established.

This makes it possible for the song to conclude in the words of the praising choir, which seem very short, but were probably repeated many times when they were sung liturgically, and were taken up in acclamations by the whole congregation:

> Yahweh is king
>   for ever and ever.

### History as the Basis of Praise

The words of the praising choir assume what is said by the narrative choir. Israel's hymn is based upon salvation history. The historical experiences contained in a narrative which is recounted in terms of images, but refers to what has taken place in history, make possible the general statements concerning the nature of Yahweh which are developed by the praising choir. Only because

Israel has experienced God's victory, God's redemption, and God's leading into the Holy Land, can it hymn its God as a hero in war, as terrible and mighty, and as him who is God, holy above all gods, and king for ever and ever. These are not abstract deductions from an assumed concept of God, but summaries of what is shown by history. Even in worship — for this hymn in fact comes from the cult — Israel encounters the true nature of God only in recalling the saving act of Yahweh experienced by the present generation or by the generations of the fathers, acts which are still present at least through the fact that Israel still lives in this sacred mountain country and even now is assembled in that very place, in Yahweh's sanctuary, to worship before him.

## The Question With Which We Began

But is the history which Israel recalls still identical with that which we recall in the worship of the New Testament, and which becomes a reality in us in baptism and the other sacraments? Have we not to turn to Christ — and not to the event at the Sea of Reeds? Or are the death and resurrection of Christ, our history of salvation, to be equated with the victory at the Sea of Reeds, the salvation history of Israel? We have returned to the question with which we began. In exegetical terms, it must be formulated as follows: is the description of salvation history recounted by the narrative choir in the song of Moses complete in itself or not? It would be complete in itself if it referred only to the events of that time, and to nothing more. It would be incomplete and open-ended, if from the very first it was planned and also understood in such a way that it is possible for later saving acts of God to be drawn into it, up to and including the death and resurrection of Christ. This question must be regarded as a question concerning the original literal meaning, for modern exegesis cannot be content with anything else.

## The Underlying Structure of the Imagery of the Hymn

My thesis is that the narrative contained in the hymn is incomplete and open-ended. Its purpose is to provide a context of imagery in which differences in time are suppressed, and into which every act of God on behalf of his chosen people can be fitted. This can be shown by continuing our exegetical analysis. Let us examine the underlying pattern of imagery which provides a hidden guiding theme in the two main texts of the narrative choir: verses 8–11 and 12–17.

Verses 8–10 describe the destruction of the enemies of Israel at the Sea of Reeds. This description clearly falls into three parts. In verse 8 and 10 Yahweh is the subject of the statement; the description is of the breath of Yahweh, which first piles up and holds still the sea, and then blows it back again. In the intervening verse 9 the enemies are the subject of the statement. Their greed drives them to pursue the Israelites through the open pathway in the sea. Behind everything lies a simple pattern of imagery: there is a narrow passage, dangers threaten on the right and the left in the form of congealed masses of water, and men attempt to pass, rapidly and compelled by their inner desire, through the dangers to the other side of the danger zone. Thus the structure of the imagery on which the text is based is that of "passage through dangers threatening." The structure is resolved in catastrophe. In the catastrophe the victory of Yahweh over his enemies is manifested.

If this fundamental pattern of imagery in the historical narrative of verses 8–10 can be established, then almost inevitably a question arises for everyone who knows the other biblical accounts of the events at the Sea of Reeds. Why is the description of the other image, the safe and successful passage of the Israelites through the same path between the waters, completely lacking from this narrative? It is a fact that the song of victory in Exodus 15 completely overlooks the passage of the Israelites through the sea. The prose narrative in Exodus 14 proceeds in a quite different way. There Yahweh divides the waters (v. 21), the Israelites pass safely through (v. 22), the Egyptians pursue them and venture between the waters (v. 23) — then follows a passage from another narrative source — and finally the waters close over the Egyptians (v. 27). The failure to mention the passage of the Israelites in the song of Exodus 15 already gave offense in biblical times. For at the end of the song a prose addition is included:

> When the horses of Pharaoh with his chariots and his horsemen went into the sea and Yahweh brought back the waters of the sea upon them, the people of Israel had walked on dry ground through the midst of the sea.

Why is this positive side of the ancient Israelite tradition of the Exodus left out of this hymn?

It has not been left out. The successful passage of Israel through the midst of the dangers which lie in wait for them is in fact described, and in a very conscious manner — but with other historical material. This is done in verses 12–17, the second lengthy passage sung by the narrative chorus. This describes how Yahweh led Israel into the land of Canaan. In the passages which form the framework (vv. 12–13 and 17), the theme is the goal toward which Israel is led, the land of Canaan; so we will turn at once to the decisive middle passage, verses 14–17.

We have already established that here Israel is presented as entering its new land as in a procession through the avenue of sphinxes. The nations, struck still by the terror of Yahweh, do not hinder Israel's passage, and cannot hold it back. It is immediately clear that the basis of the narrative is the same pattern of imagery as in verses 8–10. Once again, a procession passes through the danger zone. But by contrast to the passage of the Egyptians through the sea, success comes at the end. The threatening masses of the nations correspond here to the masses of water on each side of the passage of the Egyptians. Just as Yahweh congeals the masses of water, so he now turns the nations to stone, so that Israel can pass between them, and they do not flow back together upon Israel. Thus there is a positive image opposed to the passage of the Egyptians through the sea — but its starting point is formed by different saving acts of Yahweh.

## The Typology of History Within the Song

This is decisive for our purpose. According to the conviction expressed in the song of Moses, the saving act of Yahweh at the

Sea of Reeds is in no sense an isolated fact existing in itself. In the first instance it has a distinctive structure, that of the leading of the people through dangers which are bound to bring ruin upon anyone else who does not have the help of Yahweh. This basic structure of a pathway which is threatened, but which is made safe by Yahweh and so leads to its goal, is also to be found in other saving acts of Yahweh, such as his leading of Israel into the land of Canaan. Thus one event can take the place of another. The passage of the Israelites through the Red Sea can be represented by the passage of the Israelites through the petrified sea of the surrounding nations.

There are no grounds for supposing that the author of the song intended the validity of this structure of God's saving acts to be limited to the two saving events mentioned. He was composing his song as a cultic hymn for all the generations of Israel which were to come. There is no doubt that he was convinced that coming generations would be able to see their own experience of Yahweh contained in this song. This was in fact the case, as later material in the Bible makes plain. The author of the book of Joshua, no doubt following the indication given in the song of Moses, describes the passage of Israel over the Jordan as a second exodus from Egypt. At a later period, the prophets expected that Yahweh would repeat his act of salvation at the exodus. Deutero-Isaiah in particular interprets the return from the exile as a new exodus. Typological references of this kind at a later period are possible, because from the very first the saving act of the exodus was not regarded as a pure isolated fact, but at the same time as a revelation, in its structure, of the way in which Yahweh always and everywhere acts with regard to Israel.

In its literal meaning, the song of Moses already was composed in such a way that later saving acts of Yahweh could be introduced and read into its account of history, reduced as it was to a few basic images. Its very structure already assumed its typological application. This, however, is always meant to apply to genuine acts of Yahweh, even though one can draw attention to the fact that the intermediate structural concept — passage through dangers to a successful goal — also reflects archetypal features of psychology and religious sociology, such as processions and rites of initiation.

### The Legitimacy of the Christian Typology of the Exodus

If the song of Moses is open, in the way we have described, to take into itself the future saving acts of Yahweh, then it is possible and indeed necessary, following God's saving act in Christ, to attempt to relate the song of Moses to this act also. At least in giving an adequate interpretation of Exodus 15 one should attempt to set out the connection between this text and the passage of Christ through his death to his resurrection. The song demands to be elucidated on a basis of these events, which were still to come when it was written. Since baptism is a genuine participation in the death and resurrection of Christ, it is also legitimate to extend the typological interpretation to Christian baptism, although the duty remains of bearing constantly in mind that this connection is mediated through the way of salvation followed by Christ. Naturally, this legitimate interpretation, based upon the literal sense of Exodus 15 itself, does not permit any frivolous and fortuitous individual comparisons, such as between the waters of the Red Sea and those of baptism, or between the Egyptian soldiers and the demons. The literal meaning of the song provides no justification for this. Within the song itself, the waters of the Sea of Reeds already are replaced by the nations of Palestine. We are not advocating any facile allegorization.

But the liturgy itself rarely goes so far. This was only done by Church Fathers and medieval theologians, whom we have no need to follow in this respect. Perhaps they did not take it so seriously themselves, but knew that they were playing. And perhaps in a closed Christian society a measure of intellectual play was permissible, something in which we can no longer indulge in the open world, repeatedly disillusioned by the presence of unbelief, in which our own faith is exercised.

However, what is decisive for us is that a modern exegesis followed consistently to its conclusion can no longer be accepted as an argument against the typological use of the song of Moses in our Easter Vigil liturgy. Rather, the text demands this spiritual interpretation. Exegesis does not do justice to the song if it ignores the typological view of the history of salvation, which belongs to the song from the very first.

An exegesis which is troubled by the discovery of a typological sense in the Old Testament, because it is honest and sensible, and often cannot see how such a conclusion is arrived at, must be respected at the present day. On the other hand, an exegesis which from the very first declares that it will have nothing to do with typology is narrow-minded. How can it know that historical method itself will not force it to return to typology?

We began with the fundamental question whether the traditional liturgy with its typological thought was still meaningful for us at the present day. In conclusion, we must point out that our study has not been sufficient to give an unqualified affirmative as an answer to this question. In the first place, we have only shown in the case of the single text that its literal meaning requires typological application. The situation might well be different with other texts. Second, it is only the difficulty with which the exegete is faced which has been removed. It could be that one might recognize that most scriptural texts were suitable for typological application, and nevertheless one could hold the opinion that liturgical typology no longer has anything to say to us. So that even if the objections of the exegete to a typological application of the scripture were to be silenced, one might still perhaps resolve to conceive of liturgy in a radically new way, which it is not yet possible for us to imagine. But this would no longer be the business of the exegete.

# CHAPTER FIVE

# THE GREAT COMMANDMENT

With the concept "the great commandment," today we immediately associate a definite content. We think of the command to love God and one's neighbor. We have in mind the passage in Mark 12:28–34, parallels to which, with some differences, are to be found in Matthew 22:34–40 and Luke 10:25–28. The text in Mark 12 reads as follows:

> (28) And one of the scribes came up and heard them disputing with one another, and seeing that he answered them well, asked him, "Which commandment is the first of all?" (29) Jesus answered, "The first is, 'Hear, O Israel: The Lord our God, the Lord is one; (30) and you shall love the Lord your God with all your heart, and with all your soul, and with all your mind, and with all your strength.' (31) The second is this, 'You shall love your neighbor as yourself.' There is no other commandment greater than these." (32) And the scribe said to him, "You are right, Teacher: you have truly said that he is one, and there is no other but he; (33) and to love him with all the heart, and with all the understanding, and with all the strength, and to love one's neighbor as oneself is much more than all whole burnt offerings and sacrifices." (34) And when Jesus saw that he answered wisely, he said to him, "You are not far from the kingdom of God."

What takes place here is quite simple. A question is posed: the question of the greatest commandment. An answer is given: the twofold commandment of love.

What takes place clearly shows that the concept of the principal commandment can be thought of without it being necessarily equated at once with love of God and one's neighbor. One can ask which commandment is the principal commandment. Thus the "great commandment" is in the first instance a purely formal concept. As such it is open to question. Jesus understands the question. It is his answer which first gives a content to the concept — and the question which preceded his answer in fact assumes that there were circumstances in which it was possible to answer it differently.

What is the meaning of the concept of the "great commandment," the content of which remained open, and which evidently existed in the environment in which Jesus lived? In Mark 12:28 the scribe asks: "Which commandment is the first of all?" Thus it is assumed here that the 248 commandments and 365 prohibitions of the Torah are not all isolated units of equal importance, but that there is some order among them. The multiplicity of the divine will which impinges upon man, surrounding him and hedging him about at the same time, is rational, and there is a hierarchy in it. There is a commandment which is the "first of all." In what sense is it the first? In his final statement, with which he concludes his answer, Jesus makes use of a second formula: "There is no other commandment greater than these" (Mark 12:31). Thus the first place among the commandments is determined by the greatness, which presumably means the importance of the commandments. In Matthew this is the main formula which is used (Matthew 22:36, 38), to which the first is added only incidentally (Mt 22:38). But in Jesus' concluding sentence in Matthew a third definition is introduced, which clarifies the definition even further: "On these two commandments depend all the law and the prophets" (Matthew 22:40).

It is perhaps less important that the "great commandment" is related here not only to the commandments of the Torah but also to the whole scripture, since in such a context both entities were presumably interchangeable. On the other hand, it is decisive that the dependence of all other utterances of the divine will upon the "first" and "greatest" is accepted. It is difficult to determine whether this relationship of dependence was thought of as a genuine relationship of derivation, or if it is merely supposed that one comprehends and underlies the content of the other. In any case, the multiplicity of the divine will is seen as an ordered whole, which possesses in the "first" and "greatest" commandment the principle of its unity. Luke contains the passage, but avoids the whole terminology (Lk 10:25: "Teacher, what shall I do to inherit eternal life?"). This shows that he could not assume that his Hellenistic readers were acquainted with it. Thus it is a concept of Palestinian Judaism. At the time of Jesus there existed the formal conception of a "great commandment," the content of which, however, was not fixed and agreed, and which Jesus took up and applied to the double commandment of the love of God and one's neighbor.

In what follows, we shall discusss something of the remote prehistory of the theology of the principal commandment. We shall be discussing facts of which Old Testament exegesis has become aware only in recent years. Texts to which little attention was given previously, especially from the Book of Deuteronomy, have been shown to be a reflection of early discussions concerning the principal commandment among the Old Testament people of God. The fixed concepts which occur in Mark and Matthew are not to be found there, but the idea is unmistakably present. In the context of the problem of the principal commandment statements appear which are not usually directly associated with the double commandment of love.

### The Pre-Israelite Origin of the Concept

The conviction of the existence of a principal commandment is not something, as we might have expected, which originated in Israel as a result of the very nature of the problem itself. Thus the situation was not that Israel found itself faced with the disturbing fact of a disordered and incoherent multiplicity of individual commandments, and then felt the need of reducing this phenomenon to an intellectual unity. Rather, Israel derived from elsewhere the conviction that there was an internal hierarchy within the commandments, and that therefore there existed a principal commandment in the context of a wider complex of concepts and utterances. Israel then applied this view to the religious material in question. We are speaking of the conception which came to underlie the institution and theology of the covenant of God with Israel.

Israel did not understand its relationship to its God as a mystical participation, as the cyclical repetition of myths about the beginning of time, or as the magical and ritual manifestation of areas of numinous power, but as a "covenant." But it is better to replace the word "covenant" by another term. Israel was of the opinion that at the beginning of its history, at Mount Sinai, its God concluded a "treaty" with his people. Naturally Israel was conscious of the limits of this conceptual model, and brought to it various correctives which served to emphasize the analogical character of the concept. And yet it was thought of in genuinely juridical terms. It was seen as a tension between two freedoms: the freedom of the one God, Yahweh, who chose Israel to be his own people from among all the nations, and the freedom of this people, taking on an obligation to Yahweh in a treaty.

What existed, however, was not merely an intellectual model, but an institution. Just as international treaties between kings were always recorded at that time in a document, so there was a "covenant document" for the treaty between Yahweh and Israel. Just as international treaties at that time had to be read publicly at regular intervals, so the covenant document was regularly read in Israel. The ceremonies of the reading of the covenant must have formed a central element of the Israelite cult, as has been mentioned elsewhere.

The will of God is also understood on the basis of the idea of a treaty. For Israel, God's commandments and laws are "covenant requirements." They are nothing other than the "conditions" of the treaty between God and his people.

The links between the religious concept of the covenant in Israel and the secular procedure of treaties at that period can be demonstrated in detail. There is a particularly close link with a distinct type of covenant relationship from the middle and late Bronze Age, the so-called vassal treaties. They play an important part in the international law of the second half of the second millennium B.C. in the Near East. Through such vassal treaties emperors (our documents derive principally from the Hittite sphere) associated with themselves smaller kingdoms on the periphery of their dominions. The style and form of the vassal treaties are well known to us from archaeological discoveries. They usually follow a fixed formula. The emperor speaks in the first person. He begins by announcing himself (giving his names and title). This announcement of himself is followed by an historical retrospect. This describes the history of the political relationships between the two partners to the treaty. Here the unreliability and disloyalty of the vassal and the loyalty and magnanimity of the emperor are set forth.

This historical prologue concluded with the situation in which the treaty is being concluded at the present moment. The emperor confirms the rule of the vassal in his own area. Then follows: "And now. . . ." This stylistic link introduced the conditions of the treaty. It is followed first of all by a kind of general clause or declaration of principle. This defines the mutual relationship of the two partners to the treaty in very general concepts. Usually it simply implies: "You are to protect me and I will protect you." Then, in the individual conditions, this basic declaration is developed and made specific. After the individual conditions follows a list of gods. The gods of the two countries are called upon as witnesses to the treaty. Finally a curse and a blessing are promised to the vassal, a curse if the treaty is broken, and a blessing if it is kept. In rough outline, this is the formula of the vassal treaties. Two copies of each treaty are drawn up, on two "treaty tables," and deposited in the principal temples of the two countries.

The correspondences in many texts of the Old Testament which relate to the covenant relationship of Israel to Yahweh are frequently striking. We need only refer to the best known of these texts, the "ten commandments." According to the descriptions in Exodus and Deuteronomy, they formed the document, drawn up in two copies, of the concluding of the covenant at Sinai. In a brief form, they follow the first half of the treaty formula. There is first the self-designation of the emperor: "I am Yahweh, your God." Then there is the historical prologue, which sets out the favors shown by the emperor: "I brought you out of the land of Egypt, out of the house of bondage." Then there is the basic demand: "You shall have no other gods before me." Finally there are the individual commandments, the list formed by the remaining commands of the Decalogue. In monotheist Israel there are naturally no lists of gods. In the case of the Decalogue, there is no blessing and curse, but they are found in similar Old Testament texts.

For the question of the "great commandment" the fixed sequence, in the literary category of the covenant formula, of the fundamental declaration and the individual requirements is important. The secular category which provides its pattern already possessed something like the formal conception of a principal commandment. Once Israel had come to understand its relationship to God as a "covenant," it would necessarily have to think in terms of a principal commandment with regard to the divine will. From the very first, in the covenant formula, Israel was provided with a pattern of thought and language in which a theology of the principal commandment was already implied. Did Israel perceive the significance of this formal structure, or did it merely continue it as an empty form? If Israel understood it, what use was made of it?

### Versions of the First Commandments Derived From Constitutional Law

The structure of the Book of Deuteronomy, the last of the great collections of law in the Pentateuch, is based upon that of the liturgical festival of the renewal of the covenant. This in its turn derives from the structure of the covenant formula. In the Book of Deuteronomy the part which contains individual commandments can be distinguished easily in chapters 12–26, while the blessing and curse come in chapter 28. In chapters 1–11 there is frequent alternation between historical retrospect and general exhortatory material, not yet referring to individual commandments. It is clear from the structure of the covenant formula that these passages of "parenesis" are nothing other than elaborations of the theme of the great commandment. Thus Israel recognized the formal function of the great commandment, and developed it in its worship. It is possible to make out Israel's theology of the principal commandment from the exhortatory passages in chapters 1–11 of Deuteronomy. It is possible to see first of all that not merely the formal structure of the secular treaty tradition, but also themes contained in it, its concepts and its formulas, were taken over and applied to the relationship of Yahweh with Israel. There are several versions of the great commandment, the form of which was not originally religious, but political.

In the Decalogue the great commandment reads: "You shall have no other gods before my face." Thus it expresses Yahweh's exclusive claim to the worship of Israel. This corresponds exactly to the basic feature of the vassal relationship. A vassal king could not set up any association with a foreign ruler. Through the treaty of vassalage he was subject to his feudal lord alone, as his emperor. Since in the early period of Israel wholly accepted the existence of "other gods" (cf. Dt 4:19; 29:25; 32:8), the correspondence here is an exact one. All other demands made by Yahweh upon Israel rest upon this "privilege" by which he has an exclusive right to Israel's worship.

A second version of Yahweh's exclusive claim is found in Deuteronomy 6:14: "You shall not go after other gods" (cf. also Dt. 8:19; 11:28; 13:3, 5; 28:14). To go behind the emperor, and to go behind him alone, was the duty of a vassal. Israel had to fulfill this duty with regard to its God. In the New Testament, Jesus' call to go after him (usually translated "follow" him) goes back to the ancient formula.

A third formulation of the great commandment which derives from the political sphere is the commandment of love itself: "You shall love Yahweh your God with all your heart, and with all your soul, and with all your might" (Dt 6:5; cf. also 5:10; 7:9; 10:12; 11:1, 13, 22; 19:9). The international law of the ancient Near East did not think, like our modern international law, in terms of relationships between abstract entities, called "states," but in terms of personal relationships between sovereigns. These relationships also can be referred to as "love." In diplomatic correspondence and in the text of treaties we find this word several times, and once even a requirement that the vassal should "love the emperor like yourself." The commandment of love, notably in the phrase added to it "with your whole heart, your whole soul and your whole might" (which likewise derives from the language of diplomacy), also expresses the exclusive claim of Yahweh upon Israel.

But all three formulas derive from the political sphere, and in their religious sense are adaptations. There is no need to emphasize that they naturally took on a far more profound connotation in the process. But it is still worthwhile to know that the different formulas originally shared a genuine common content. They were only restored to their original unity when Jesus later took them up and applied them to himself. He made the demand to love him and to follow him. The ancient link between the commandment of love and law reappears in the New Testament in a place where it is perhaps least to be expected — in the Johannine theology: "He who has my commandments and keeps them, he it is indeed who loves me" (Jn 14:21; cf. also Jn 14:15, 23; 2:3–5).

## New Israelite Formulations of the Great Commandment Based Upon the Cult

Israel was ready to formulate the great commandment anew, if the needs of the moment demanded it. There was no difficulty in this process in leaving behind the sphere from which the formulations were originally derived, that of international law. This can be seen in the example of the Decalogue.

The first formulation of the great commandment is followed by two others. As far as we can tell, they do not belong to the oldest text of the Decalogue, but were added in the course of time by the Israelite authorities, with the obvious intention of adapting the great commandment to the changed needs of the time.

The first is the addition which immediately follows the older formula; it reads, "You shall not make for yourself a graven image, or any likeness of anything that is in heaven above, or that is on the earth beneath, or that is in the water under the earth" (Dt 5:8 = Ex 20:4). Here, then, the setting up of images of God is forbidden. This expresses in more concrete terms the ancient form of the great commandment. It reflects a situation in which there was present a particularly powerful influence from pagan civilization, perhaps during a period of foreign rule.

The second reformulation of the great commandment contained in the Decalogue reads, "You shall not bow down to them or serve them" (Dt 5:9 = Ex 20:5). The twofold expression "bow down to them or serve them" is never used in the older books of the Bible for the worship of the true God. Rather, it reflects a heathen rite, that of casting oneself down in worship before the image of a god, the details of which we no longer know, but which makes very clear the great temptation of Israel at certain moments of its history, that of apostasy from Yahweh.

Thus the prohibition of the setting up of images of gods and of this pagan rite are not meant as individual commandments, following upon the great commandment of the Decalogue, but as reformulations of the great commandment itself. This is clear from the fact that the sentence which provides the motive for the principal commandment does not occur until after the new versions. This sentence also clearly refers to the exclusive claim of Yahweh. Furthermore, it refers to the second ancient formulation of the great commandment, that which contains the concept of the love of God: "For I Yahweh your God am a jealous God, visiting the iniquity of the fathers upon the children to the third and fourth generation of those who hate me, but showing steadfast love to thousands of those who love me and keep my commandments" (Dt 5:9 f. = Ex 20:5 f). Only after the motives for the great commandment have been given in this way, do the individual commandments of the Decalogue follow.

That both the commandments which follow the oldest version of the great commandment were regarded as genuine versions of the great commandment also can be seen from chapter 4 of Deuteronomy. Deuteronomy 4:1–40 is a sermon intended to inculcate the observance of the great commandment and so of the whole law. After a long introductory exhortation, there follows a description of the appearance of God on Sinai. Particular emphasis is laid on the fact that while the people of Israel heard the voice of God on Sinai, they saw no visible form. This serves as a justification for the prohibition of the setting up of images, and of the carrying out of heathen rites before the sun and the moon and the stars, as can be seen from the words which directly follow it:

> "Therefore take good heed to yourselves. Since you saw no form on that day that Yahweh spoke to you at Horeb out of the midst of the fire, beware lest you act corruptly by making a graven image for yourselves, in the form of any figure, the likeness of male or female, the likeness of any beast that is on the earth, the likeness of any winged bird that flies in the air, the likeness of anything that creeps on the ground, the likeness of any fish that is in the water under the earth. And beware lest you lift up your eyes to heaven, and when you see the sun and the moon and the stars, all the host of heaven, you be drawn away and worship them and serve them" (Dt 4:15–19).

If one looks more closely, one realizes that the whole wording of the two additional versions which follow the ancient great commandment of the Decalogue forms the framework on which this text is based, and about which everything else is ranged as a commentary. On the other hand, all reference to the ancient version of the great commandment (to have no "other gods") is completely lacking in 4:1–40. Thus the term in 4:1–40 regards the two consciously cultic formulations of the great commandment as the only ones which provided a decisive standard for its own time.

### The Fear of God as the Great Commandment

In addition to the cultic course followed by the further development of the great commandment, there is another, which seems more concerned with the underlying religious attitude. This was thought of in the ancient East as the "fear" of the gods. In accordance with this, the great commandment can be formulated or at least interpreted as a commandment to "fear" Yahweh alone. This takes place in a commentary, the structure of which is similar to that in Deuteronomy 4:15–19. In this case, the basis is provided by the beginning of the Decalogue in its original form, that is, without the cultic reformulation of the great commandment. This proceeds from the point at which Yahweh announces himself to the beginning of the sentence which provides the motive for the commandment. The commentary is found in Deuteronomy 6:12–15:

> "Take heed lest you forget Yahweh, who brought you out of the land of Egypt, out of the house of bondage. You shall fear Yahweh your God; you shall serve him, and swear by his name. You shall not go after other gods, of the gods of the people who are around about you; for Yahweh your God in the midst of you is a jealous God; lest the anger of Yahweh your God be kindled against you, and he destroy you from off the face of the earth."

The decisive key words in this commentary are "to fear," "to serve," and "to swear by the name of God." To serve and to swear refer to cultic actions. But the decisive word is "to fear." For Deuteronomy 6: 12–15 forms an integral part of the more extensive sermon comprising chapters 5 and 6 (at the beginning which, in Chapter 5, the whole Decalogue is quoted within this sermon). In this longer text the dominant theme is the "fear" of God. Deuteronomy 5:5 declares that Israel was afraid at the sight of the theophany on Sinai. The appearance of God in the fire gave Israel the experience of trembling awe before the divine mystery which is a part of every religious experience. In this experience man feels that he is at the threshold between life and death. His whole existence is called into question in the face of infinite being. This is expressed in the proposal made by the people in Deuteronomy 5:24–27, that God should no longer deal with them directly, but only through the mediation of Moses.

Yahweh gives Moses the following answer to this: "Oh that they had such a mind as this always, to fear me and to keep all my commandments, that it might go well with them and with their children for ever!" (Dt 5:29).

In the following verses the idea of the fear of Yahweh is mentioned several times to characterize the nature of the great commandment. The remarkable mutual relationship between the fear of Yahweh and the observance of all Yahweh's commandments becomes clear. On the one hand, the observance of all the commandments comes from the fear of Yahweh (Dt 6:2), while on the other hand Israel is to observe all the commandments, in order to fear Yahweh thereby (Dt 6:24). Thus the fear of Yahweh and the observance of the individual commandments support each other, and this makes it clear that the fear of Yahweh is not an individual commandment, but is concerned with the content of the great commandment.

By comparison with cultic categories of the new formulae within the Decalogue, the "fear of Yahweh" in the interpretation of the great commandment in chapters 5 and 6 is certainly a step forward. It touches the essence of the matter. But we must note that here too what is decisive is not that this basic religious attitude is approved, but that it is concentrated entirely upon Yahweh, the one and only God of Israel.

### The Great Commandment in the Situation of Prosperity

At a later period Deuteronomy 8 was composed. This chapter is presented as a commentary upon the comment on the great commandment of Deuteronomy 6, which was mentioned previously. Here it is the term "forget" to which particular attention is paid, a term which occurs at the very beginning of the commentary in Deuteronomy 6: "Take heed lest you forget Yahweh, who brought you out of the land of Egypt, out of the house of bondage" (Dt 6:12). This theme is elaborated in Chapter 8 with a length and fullness which is no doubt late in date. The text is meant for a condition of prosperity. Deuteronomy 8:7–9 describes the beauty, fertility and richness of the land in which Israel dwells. Israel has food and drink, is satisfied, builds beautiful houses and lives in them, while cattle and sheep multiply, silver and gold pile up, and possessions of every kind increase (Dt 8:10, 12, 13). In this situation, Israel is exhorted to take heed lest it forget Yahweh (Dt 8:11). This warning is then developed:

> "Lest . . . then your heart be lifted up, and you forget Yahweh your God, . . . lest you say in your heart, 'My power and the might of my hand have gotten me this wealth.' You shall remember Yahweh your God, for it is he who gives you power to get wealth . . ." (Dt. 8:14, 17, 18).

The temptation of Israel to which this refers no longer consists of the worship of other gods, the splendor of images and the ecstacy of pagan cults. The danger that threatens here can be recognized as that of secularization. Even the praise of God in the cult becomes a routine, which is not carried out any longer from the heart (Dt 8:10 f. should be translated as follows: "And when you have eaten and are full, and bless Yahweh your God for the good land he has given you" — this refers to Israel's worship — "then take heed, lest you forget Yahweh your God . . ."). With reference to this forgetting, which is becoming increasingly widespread in the process of the secularization of existence, the demand of the great commandment is now formulated as "remember." The most important thing is seen as restoring the consciousness of the reality of God. The observance of all other commandments will result from this.

### The Great Commandment for the Devout and for Those Who Observe the Law

Even in an Israel, which remembers its God and ascribes its prosperity wholly to him, a final danger is still present, which is capable of perverting everything once again. It is that of the observance of all the commandments, and the resulting consciousness of one's own righteousness in the sight of God. In this situation the great commandment becomes as it were the dialectical antithesis to the observance of the commandments. It unmasks danger of the loss of God, which is still present even when all the commandments are observed, and forces men to look only upon God himself, and not upon their own good actions. This is done in a text at the beginning of Deuteronomy 9.

This text, however, makes use of imagery which was already archaic at the time at which it was composed, because in accord-

ance with the whole stylization of Deuteronomy, it is intended
to be understood as a statement by Moses before the entry into
the promised land. Moses promises that with the help of God,
Israel will conquer the whole land in an unparalleled campaign
of conquest. And if it is to be possible to see and experience the
assistance of God in this way, then Israel must remember:

> "Do not say in your heart, after Yahweh your God has
> thrust them out before you, 'It is because of my righteous-
> ness that Yahweh has brought me to possess this land';
> whereas it is because of the wickedness of these nations
> that Yahweh is driving them out before you. Not because
> of the righteousness or the unrightness of your heart are
> you going in to possess their land; but because of the
> wickedness of these nations Yahweh your God is driving
> them out from before you, and that he may confirm the
> word which Yahweh swore to your fathers, to Abraham,
> to Isaac and to Jacob. Know, therefore, that Yahweh
> your God is not giving you this good land to possess
> because of your righteousness; for you are a stubborn
> people" (Dt 9:4–6).

Then, to demonstrate how stiff-necked Israel is, Moses lists
all the sins which Israel has committed in forty years wandering
in the wilderness. The list concludes with 9:23 f.:

> "When Yahweh sent you from Kadesh-barnea, saying,
> 'Go up and take possession of the land which I have
> given you,' then you rebelled against the commandment
> of Yahweh your God, and did not believe him or obey
> his voice. You have been rebellious against Yahweh
> from the day that I knew you."

Here the key word is the "righteousness" of Israel. It is thought
of as a righteousness coming from the observance of the law.
It is passionately rejected. If Israel believes that it is righteous
through the observance of the law, and that the blessing of God
which it obtains is a reward for its own uprightness of heart, this
is false. Israel is not righteous. Israel is stiff-necked and has a
rebellious heart. This is the reality of Israel, to whom nevertheless the blessing of Yahweh is accorded. Its ultimate basis is
solely the freedom of God, the freedom with which he promised

this blessing to the patriarchs. If situations exist in which Israel lives in the constant glow of God's blessing, and has the impression that its observance of the law has really deserved this reward, the great commandment meets these situations by taking the form of the prohibition of pride in Israel's own righteousness.

Here, therefore, in the middle of the Old Testament, and indeed in the middle of the "law" of the Old Testament, stands a typically Pauline statement. Thus even the Pauline themes of faith and works, of the righteousness of God and man's own righteousness on the basis of the fulfillment of the law, grew up in the context of reflection upon the "great commandment." For there can be no doubt that Paul is dependent upon this text.

## The Great Commandment in the New Treatment

At this point we shall break off our study of the Old Testament. The "great commandment" as a category was found in Israel from the very first, embedded in the theology of the covenant. As far as its content was concerned, Israel retained the freedom to rephrase the great commandment, to bring it into accordance with contemporary needs. In the first part of the Book of Deuteronomy, a broad path can be traced from the first formulas, adopted from international law, to what is virtually a "Pauline" statement. The new formulations, however, do not replace the old, as can be seen by the fact that they stand in peaceful juxtaposition in the final text of Deuteronomy.

The fact that different texts coexist and are interwoven in this way, however, also shows that what ultimately matters is not the way the great commandment is formulated at any particular time, but what at the beginning of our study was called the formal aspect of it. This means that there actually does exist a unity of the divine will, that the multiplicity of God's commands are rooted in a single basic command, that all lead back to it, and that the encounter between man and God is ultimately something simple. What is the special contribution of the New Testament to this Old Testament doctrine of the unity of the divine will?

It is not that a further formulation is now added to those which already existed. As far as its content is concerned, the New

Testament simply draws upon the Old. This is never made more clear than in the agreement between Jesus and the scribe with regard to the twofold commandment of love: "You are right, Teacher; you have truly spoken" (Mk 12:32). But the New Testament does not merely draw upon the commandment of love, but also on most of the other formulations. In addition to the theme of love, we also have the theme of following and that of the rejection of one's own righteousness. The themes which were begun in the Old Testament were simply taken further.

Thus what is new in the New Testament does not consist of the formal and conceptual aspect. Basically it consists only of one thing: everything is now no longer referred to God, but to Jesus of Nazareth, in whom God became present in the world. Where the demand was earlier made to Israel, not to go after other gods, but after Yahweh, Jesus now says, "Follow me." At the heart of Paul's rejection of man's own righteousness there stands the doctrine of justification by faith, brought about by the death and the resurrection of Jesus Christ. The new commandment which Jesus gave against the background of the old commandment of the love of God is the commandment to love him, and to love the brethren in the love of him.

"The great commandment" therefore signifies fundamentally that the will of God does not hedge us around in an oppressing and confusing multiplicity, but is ultimately a unity, in such a way that all particular expressions of the divine will all depend upon this one basic will, derive from it and are comprehended in it, regardless of whether in a given situation this basic will is described in concrete terms. But in the New Testament "the great commandment" means, in addition to this, that what ultimately matters is the relationship of man with Christ.

# CHAPTER SIX

# LAW AND GRACE

The heart of the Old Testament is the Pentateuch, which consists for the most part of laws. They are embedded in an historical narrative, but they so dominate it, that Jewish tradition calls the Pentateuch the *torah*, that is, the law. Psalm 19:8–11 says of this law:

> The law of the Lord is perfect,
>   reviving the soul;
> the testimony of the Lord is sure,
>   making wise the simple;
> the precepts of the Lord are right,
>   rejoicing the heart;
> the commandment of the Lord is pure,
>   enlightening the eyes;
> the fear of the Lord is clean,
>   enduring forever;
> the ordinances of the Lord are true,
>   and righteous altogether.
> More to be desired are they than gold,
>   even much fine gold;
> sweeter also than honey
>   and drippings of the honeycomb.

The law appears as the concrete form of the grace of God toward men. How different this is from what Paul says about the same law in Chapter 3 of the Epistle to the Galatians:

> If the inheritance is by the law, it is no longer by promise; but God gave it to Abraham by a promise.

103

Why then the law? It was added because of transgressions, till the offspring should come to whom the promise had been made . . . if a law had been given which could make alive, then righteousness would indeed be by the law. But the scripture consigned all things to sin, that what was promised to faith in Jesus Christ might be given to those who believe. Now before faith came, we were confined under the law, kept under restraint until faith should be revealed. So that the law was our custodian until Christ came, that we might be justified by faith. But now faith has come, we are no longer under a custodian (Gal 3:18–25).

According to Paul the law is good, but does not contain in itself the power to give men help to fulfill it. If it meets sin, it is changed into a means to sin, and effects new sin. In Israel the condition which it met was always one of sin. Consequently according to God's plan, it had only one significance in the history of salvation, that of exposing sin. In the last phase before Christ it was intended to manifest openly sins which were already present but concealed, so that the salvation promised to Abraham might come through justification by faith in Christ.

Thus here we have two completely different evaluations of the Mosaic law. They face the Christian interpreter of the Old Testament with a serious problem. How should he expound the statements of Israel, often so enthusiastic, concerning the saving action of God, his grace, his love, his choosing of Israel, the easiness of the law and the joy of man in God's will and ordinances, if all this is a deception, and Israel was only being driven deeper and deeper into sin by God, by the aid of his ordinances?

Does not the word of God contradict itself here? We are dealing here not with some marginal statement of the Bible, but both in the Old Testament, in the case of the high value placed upon the law, and also in Paul, with his rejection of the law for the sake of pure faith, with the central point of their message.

Ultimately, as a Christian, the side one takes is that of Paul. Paul speaks from the experience of Christ, which brings into question everything that proceeds it. This is the ultimate standard.

But before drawing the consequences of such a decision, one must reflect on the matter with great care. The study which follows is meant to assist such a reflection, and not to do more. It is not intended as an attack upon Paul. But it is intended to prevent us from labeling, hastily and thoughtlessly, large and decisive portions of the Old Testament as "legalist" and paying no further attention to them.

This is not to deny that the Pauline evaluation of the law already has roots in the Old Testament. The prophetic message of the final abrogation of the old covenant and the promise of the new covenant in particular presumably had its effect upon Paul. There is much more besides this. The historical vision of the Yahwist, who sees the whole world as surrounded by darkness, with the light of blessing shining on Israel alone, must have had a powerful influence upon Paul. Furthermore, the Yahwist already saw the first sin in paradise as arising out of a legal prohibition — compare this with Paul in Chapter 7 of Romans: "I should not have known what it is to covet if the law had not said, 'You shall not covet.'"

Many later passages in the Old Testament contrast the covenant with Abraham or the promises to Abraham with the covenant of Sinai, and this prepares for the way in which Paul relates sin to the law and grace and faith to Abraham. The concept of "one's own righteousness" is already developed in Deuteronomy 9. Ezekiel 20:25 makes the statement, without parallel in the Old Testament, that Yahweh gave Israel "statutes that were not good and ordinances by which they could not have life." The Pauline theology of the law is much more rooted in the Old Testament, and much less revolutionary than is usually accepted.

Nevertheless, the overwhelming fact is that the Old Testament, in the worship by which it lives and in the passages which are the true foundation of the books of the Old Testament and provide its essential form, speaks in a wholly non-Pauline manner of the law. The scholarship of recent years has made these contradictions even more clear. We go on here to give an outline of some of the results of this study.

### The Theology of the Law From Which the Pentateuch Derives

In 1940 the Protestant Old Testament scholar M. Noth published a study entitled *Die Gesetze im Pentateuch — ihre Voraussetzungen und ihr Sinn* (The Laws in the Pentateuch — their assumptions and their meaning). Noth began by asking which was the social reality with which the laws of the Pentateuch were associated. The answer was that they were not associated with anything which took the form of a state, but with the constitution of the sacral federation of tribes known as "Isreal." Here "Israel" was understood as a social reality coming under the blessing of Yahweh. Israel was founded by Yahweh's historical actions, and had henceforth existed in the form of the "covenant" with Yahweh. Within this framework, Israel's laws constituted the legal ordinance of the federation.

A previous human achievement, in the form of the observance of these laws, was in no sense a necessary condition for the coming into being of the sacred reality of Israel. When Israel did not yet exist, its laws also did not exist. God first acted and set up the sacred reality of Israel. Only then were the laws given to protect this primary reality. This order, both of the origin and the function of the law, remained throughout the course of history. In the covenant worship which regularly took place, Israel was constantly placed anew within the sphere of grace, and within this sphere, the demands of God were then proclaimed anew. With regard to their content, these "laws" had above all the intention of guarding Israel against falling away from the ordinances of grace. Consequently, the typical laws of Israel are those which directly or indirectly protect the exclusive claim of Yahweh. Basically this means the prohibition of the worship of other gods, and in the laws which apply this to particular cases, it means laws such as the prohibition of sacrificing or eating pigs — for this law protects Israel from certain Canaanite cultic practices.

According to Noth, the law ceased at the Babylonian exile to be embedded in the wider institution of grace for "Israel." The individual institutions of the people of God on which it was based collapsed, and the prophets declared that the covenant had come to an end. But since the post-exilic community nevertheless continued to cling to the old law, it was now isolated from the original setting which had nourished and surrounded it, and became an entity in itself. After the exile, obedience to the law was no longer the means of remaining within the grace which already had been given, but became a human achievement, necessary in the first place for the reception of grace. Noth believes that this new attitude to the law is already reflected in the priestly writing in the Pentateuch, and also in the hymns on the law in the Psalter. It is here, in the early stages of Judaism, that according to Noth the new law became what Paul was later to attack, whereas Paul's criticism could not be made against the pre-exilic law.

However, Noth's view of the theology of the law in the post-exilic period soon met with opposition. Wolff and Kraus disagreed with his interpretation of the hymns on the law in the Psalter, and his interpretation of the theology of the law in the priestly writing was also corrected in an essay by Zimmerli. We may leave open the question whether the time during which Paul was growing up the evaluation of the law which he attacked did in fact exist in Judaism. For the Old Testament, it can be affirmed that in the period which it represents, the laws of the Pentateuch were regarded not as the means to obtain the blessing of God in a legalist way, but as the sacred ordinance of the saving reality of the people of God which already had been given by God in his grace.

The knowledge we have concerning the institution of the covenant in Israel, mentioned on several occasions in previous chapters, has added a further dimension to the analysis made by Noth in 1940. It is true that the parallel drawn with the practice of political treaties has made the legal character of the covenant with God even more clear. But the form of a vassal treaty in the ancient Near East is that of a treaty relationship of a special structure, which in a manner of speaking includes the idea of grace. The treaty document begins with an historical prologue. This testifies to the gratuitous act of good will on the part of the emperor which proceeded the concluding of the treaty.

Yahweh chose the fathers, took Israel from Egypt, and led the people into the promised land. Through the carrying out of these acts by God, Israel became the people of Yahweh and he became Israel's God. Only after the historical preface to the covenant document has affirmed that Yahweh's grace came first, does the list of Yahweh's demands upon Israel begin. The Decalogue gives a very concise example of this. It speaks first of Yahweh's grace: "I am Yahweh your God, who brought you out of the land of Egypt, out of the house of bondage." Only then does the first commandment follow. We find the same structure, set out in baroque profusion, in the general layout of the Book of Deuteronomy. There the proclaiming of the law begins with Chapter 12, but it is preceded by sermons on the saving acts of God which have founded the covenant, and on the basic duty to be loyal to the covenant and to love God. In Israel's worship, in accordance with the form of a vassal treaty, the proclaiming of the law was followed by the pronouncing of the blessing and the curse upon Israel. But the blessing was not understood as a merited legal reward for the achievement of obedience to the law, but consisted simply of remaining and being prosperous in the saving gift which already existed before any individual fulfilled the law, the gift of the land given by Yahweh to Israel. When the possibility of being driven from the land is mentioned as the content of the curse which would apply if the covenant were broken, this signifies the loss of the saving gift already given, not the refusal of something which had to be earned through the works of the law. Paul naturally also mentions in his preaching such a possibility of losing the salvation given in grace.

### The Theology of the Law and the Deuteronomic History

I start with the hypothesis worked out by M. Noth, that of a "Deuteronomic history" composed as a single work at the beginning of the Babylonian exile, and extending from Deuteronomy to 2 Kings. In considering the message proclaimed by this history, G. von Rad and H. W. Wolff have since critically examined Noth's views and proposed certain additions to them. The work was composed when the history of Israel had come to an end. Just as this history began with the leading of Israel to the borders of the promised land under Moses and into the land under Joshua, it seemed that its end had been reached when the Northern Kingdom and then Judah and Jerusalem were exiled from this land. This history is now examined in retrospect. The question which the whole work seeks to answer is how this could come about. The question whether the history of Israel will continue, and how it can continue, is raised only very tentatively.

The "Deuteronomist," as the author of this history may be called, uses an unambiguous standard by which to judge history. This is the "book of the law" or "the book of the law of Moses." This is the usual translation. One could also term it "the covenant document" or "the Mosaic covenant document." Not only is this covenant document frequently mentioned, but also — in order to avoid any lack of clarity — it is completely incorporated into the history itself. For as far as we can tell, Deuteronomy 5–28 is the covenant document of the institution of the covenant as it existed in Jerusalem toward the end of the period of the kings. It contains Yahweh's will for Israel.

We must note here that the Deuteronomist in no sense regards the different commandments as standing all upon the same level. In practice, he measures Israel's faithfulness to the covenant by the standard of the small number of central ordinances associated with the first commandment. For him the decisive issue is the exclusive worship of Yahweh. After the temple has been built, this is supplemented by the commandment to worship Yahweh, henceforth in the cult of Jerusalem alone. In addition to the concrete will of Yahweh, the covenant document incorporated into the Deuteronomic history also contains, in the blessings and curses of Deuteronomy 28, oracles of Yahweh which point to the future, and which make the destiny of Israel in the promised land dependent upon its faithfulness to the covenant.

When the Deuteronomist measured the behavior and the faith of his people against this standard, he was forced to the following conclusion: Israel had constantly and increasingly failed to observe God's demands in the covenant. Consequently Yahweh had rightly brought into operation the curses of the covenant. The salvation which Yahweh had given through his grace at the beginning of the history of Israel had been wholly lost. Israel could only reproach itself for this, and not Yahweh. As a preface to his work, the Deuteronomist describes in Chapter 1 the fate of the first generations in the desert, those who had come out of Egypt with Moses. Because of the sin of unbelief they were condemned to die outside the promised land (Dt 1:32). This is no doubt meant to be symbolic of the whole history of Israel. In the summaries of history in 2 Kings 17 and 21 the Deuteronomist expresses the same ideas in theoretical and retrospective terms. The curse of the law has gradually accumulated against Israel and has now been released upon it.

At this point our question arises. Is the "book of the law of Moses" regarded by the Deuteronomist as "law" in the Pauline sense, which does not impart life, but drives deeper into sin and serves only to bring all men together under sin? Here again, the answer must be that it is not.

After the last generation in the wilderness had died out, the Deuteronomist presents his history as beginning with a pure generation. Only those who at the time of the unfaithfulness in the wilderness were still children were allowed to enter the promised land. Deuteronomy 2:14–17 expresses this in solemn terms:

> The time for our leaving Kadesh-barnea until we crossed the brook Zered was thirty-eight years, until the entire generation, that is, the men of war, had perished from the camp, as the Lord had sworn to them. For indeed the hand of the Lord was against them, to destroy them from the camp, until they had perished. So when all the men of war had perished and were dead from among the people, the Lord said to me . . . (cf. also Dt 1:39.)

Despite all his pleading, even Moses was not allowed to enter the promised land (cf. Dt 3:23–27). One could scarcely express more clearly in narrative terms the fact that the history of Israel in the promised land began with a pure generation. The law was not promulgated to sinners, but to an untainted people to whom, from his grace alone, God was giving a beautiful country in which to observe his will.

In the course of the history of Israel there was also the possibility of forgiveness and the renewal of Israel in the covenant. This is made particularly clear in the presentation of the period of the judges. This follows several cycles, the inner pattern of which is given in theoretical terms by the Deuteronomist in Judges 2:10 ff. A period of faithfulness to the covenant is followed by a period in which Israel lapses. Then the anger of Yahweh is kindled against them, and he brings the people into distress and oppression. In this situation the Israelites "cry" once again to Yahweh. He then has mercy and sends them a savior, called a "judge." This is the beginning of the next cycle.

Must we not say that through Yahweh's mercy, grace repeatedly flows into history and prevents the curse of the law from operating to the full? This cyclical theory cannot be reconciled with the Pauline statements that the law of Moses was only there in order to drive men deeper into sin until the coming of Christ. The period of the kings, however, is no longer divided into cyclical periods. But Wolff has shown that it is the intention of the Deuteronomist that we should regard it as the first half of a single great cycle, which at the moment at which the work is written still remains to be continued in the future.

This is the message of the history to those who read it in exile: it challenges them to bring into operation the next act of the cycle. They are to "cry" to Yahweh, and so to achieve the "return" with which a new act of Yahweh's grace begins.

At the end of Solomon's prayer at the consecration of the temple the Deuteronomist refers to this very possibility for the future:

> If they sin against thee — for there is no man who does not sin — and thou art angry with them, and dost give them to an enemy, so that they are carried away captive to the land of the enemy, far off or near; yet if they lay it to heart in the land to which they have been carried captive, and repent, and make supplication to thee in the land of their captors, saying, "We have sinned, and have acted perversely and wickedly"; if they repent with all their mind and with all their heart in the land of their enemies, who carried them captive, and pray to thee toward their land, which thou gavest to their fathers,

the city which thou hast chosen, and the house which I
have built for thy name; then hear thou in heaven thy
dwelling place their prayer and their supplication, and
maintain their cause and forgive thy people who have
sinned against thee, and all their transgressions which
they have committed against thee; and grant them compassion in the sight of those who carried them captive,
that they may have compassion on them (for they are
thy people, and thy heritage, which thou didst bring
out of Egypt, from the midst of the iron furnace) . . .
(Kg 8:46–51.)

If one bears in mind the presence of God's grace in this way at
the origin, throughout the course, and at the end of the history
described by the Deuteronomist, a history which still remains
to be completed, one can scarcely say that he saw the meaning
contained in it as the pursuing and compelling of Israel into sin,
carried out by means of the law. His history proclaims the gospel
of the gracious God, albeit with the restraint and tentativeness
which was appropriate to the gloomy situation at the exile.

Within this fundamental message of grace, the will of God
formulated in the law naturally remains an ambivalent entity,
having regard to the blessing and cursing texts associated with it.
When Israel fulfills the will of God, it continues to have the
"rest," which consists of the peaceful possession of the land,
whereas when Israel lapses, it falls under judgment, until it cries
out once again for grace.

For the Deuteronomist the figure of David is the outstanding
example of one who walks wholly in the will of Yahweh. G. von
Rad has made this abundantly clear, although he is not right in
regarding the promise of Nathan to David as a principle guiding
the force of history, independent and subject to no conditions,
which can be equated with the conditional covenant, or even
regarded as superior to it, and which can be considered separately.
It is certainly not right to describe the covenant in Pauline terms
as "the law" and the promise of Nathan by contrast as "the
gospel." The perfect obedience of David and the blessing which
flows out upon him and his house belong rather within the sphere

of the covenant, and the will of God laid down in the law is effective in him too.

Finally, it can be said of the Deuteronomic history that it applies the theology of the law inherent in the idea of the covenant and in the institution of the covenant, in its practical form. Since the history was composed during the greatest crisis of God's covenant with Israel, it lays particular emphasis on the darker possibilities of the law. Nevertheless the covenant is always regarded as the product of the divine grace at work in history. The law always functions within it. It never has the negative function in the history of salvation which Paul gave to it.

### The Attitude of the Prophets to the Law
### According to the Deuteronomic History

Prophets often appear in the Deuteronomic history. They are one of the forces which, according to this history, carry forward the history of salvation. How is what they do related to the law?

The key text to this is 2 Kings 17:7 ff. It first affirms the sin of Israel:

> This was so, because the people of Israel had sinned against the Lord their God, who had brought them up out of the land of Egypt from under the hand of Pharaoh king of Egypt, and had feared other gods and walked in the customs of the nations whom the Lord drove out before the people of Israel, and in the customs which the kings of Israel had introduced.

Thus without a law, the people cannot live at all. If it does not live according to the law of Yahweh, then it must live according to a human law, that of other nations, or that which its own kings impose upon it. If Israel follows such a law, it sins directly, through the law itself. The worst sins of Israel are now listed:

> The people of Israel did secretly against the Lord their God things that were not right. They built for themselves high places at all their towns, from watchtower to fortified city; they set up for themselves pillars and Asherim on every high hill and under every green tree; and there they burnt incense on all the high places, as

the nations did whom the Lord carried away before them. And they did wicked things, provoking the Lord to anger, and they served idols, of which the Lord had said to them, "You shall not do this."

This describes unequivocally the situation in which the covenant is broken. It is this situation which provokes the context for the task of the prophet. Consequently, the passage goes on to speak of the prophets:

Yet the Lord disputed with Israel and Judah by every prophet and every seer, saying, "Turn from your evil ways and keep my commandments and my statutes, in accordance with all the law which I commanded your fathers, and which I sent to you by my servants the prophets."

It is not necessary to quote this text further. When Israel failed to fulfill its duties under the covenant, Yahweh sent the prophets. They were his representatives, and in his name began a kind of trial with Israel, by which they attempted to move Israel to repent and to renew the observance of the covenant obligations which it had undertaken. Thus the task of the prophets is defined entirely within the framework of the covenant.

But the place of the prophets is not merely within the situation where the covenant is endangered by Israel's breaking it. The last sentence quoted above — 2 Kings 17:13 — continues. It does not mention only the "law which I commanded your fathers," but goes on to define the "law" in a second way. It is the "law which I commanded your fathers, and which I sent to you by my servants the prophets." Thus before they have to insist upon the observance of the law of the covenant, which already has been given, the prophets are also primary mediators of the law. But here the prophetic mediation of the law is distinguished from that which has been vouchsafed to the fathers. This presumably means the original making of the covenant at Sinai. Recent scholarship has revealed the idea of a prophetic office which consisted of revising and extending the covenant law. In Deuteronomy 18:14 ff., a prophet like Moses is foretold, and the obvious meaning is that Israel will always have a prophet who, like Moses, will be in a position to mediate the divine law.

A further task of the prophets is shown in the Deuteronomic history, in connection with the renewal of the covenant by Josiah. The lost covenant document was found again in the temple. Then King Josiah recognized that the covenant had been broken and carried out penitential rites (2 Kg 22:11). Then he sent a deputation to a prophetess. What she said in the name of Yahweh can be read in 2 Kings 22:15–20. This prophetic oracle must be understood in the sense that it contains Yahweh's authorization to proceed with the renewal of the covenant, which Josiah in fact then carried out (2 Kg 23:1–3).

In the Deuteronomic history other functions of the prophets also can be seen, which are not linked retrospectively and directly to the covenant and the law in the same way. But it is clear, nevertheless, that the Deuteronomist regarded the prophets as essentially Yahweh's plenipotentiaries sent to his covenant partner Israel. Depending upon the situation, their task was to clarify and extend the law of the covenant, to demand a return to faithfulness to the covenant, in the case of disobedience to name the punishment it had brought about, but in the case of repentance to give authority for the renewal of the covenant in the name of Yahweh. Thus the relation of prophecy to the law is extraordinarily close.

We already know the Deuteronomist's theology of the law. If the picture of the prophets given by the Deuteronomist is accurate, then the prophets entirely share his view of the law. This means that even the prophets had a different view of the law from that which Paul was to advance later. The question is, whether an analysis of the prophetic writings confirms this.

### Ezekiel's Attitude to the Law

The judgment made by critical scholars upon the prophets was for a long time determined by the views of Wellhausen. According to him the prophets were anterior to the law, both in time and with regard to their message — the law was a late phenomenon. The study of the prophets at the present day is in the process of refuting this view. Here the biblical theory which finds its expression in the Deuteronomic history is essentially justified.

That is, the prophets assume the covenant (and the law, in the context of the covenant), and must be understood on the basis of it.

With respect to the writing prophets, who are the most accessible to us, this is more or less true in one way or another. None is entirely an exception to this. The study of the subject is still very fluid. Different lines of study frequently run parallel but unrelated. A genuinely satisfactory and therefore widely accepted picture of the prophets is not yet available to us, however certain it may be that the idea of great individuals who founded "ethical monotheism" was an error. Nevertheless, one can affirm without hesitation the relationship of the prophets to the law.

Since it is not possible to examine each individual prophet in any detail here, let us choose one prophet whose background lies in traditions in Israel which were remote from those of Deuteronomy. This is Ezekiel. That Ezekiel's understanding of himself derives from the covenant law is at once evident from his vocation vision.

As Zimmerli has shown, the vocation vision of Ezekiel (Ezek 1:1–3:15) follows a traditional pattern. The prophet finds himself first in Yahweh's council, where Yahweh is enthroned, and is sent from this council as a messenger to Yahweh's covenant people Israel. Behind this pattern of prophetic vocation experiences we can still recognize the secular model. An emperor has a treaty with a vassal; he learns that the vassal is preparing to defect; he calls together the royal council and from the council sends a diplomatic embassy to the vassal, to influence him in the direction the emperor wishes, and to keep him loyal to the treaty. The ambassador who is sent corresponds to the prophet in Israel.

In the vocation vision of Ezekiel the ancient pattern still can be clearly recognized. But it already has been very simplified and overlaid with other features. This shows that the prophet's understanding of himself which it implies was an ancient one at his time, and was taken for granted. Ezekiel was not the first to introduce it.

Nevertheless, when Ezekiel wishes, he is still able to speak very precisely in the terms of the original secular model. This is so especially in 2:3–5. We quote the text in its reconstructed original form:

> Son of man, I send you to the people of Israel, who are rebellious against me. You shall say to them, "Thus says the Lord God" And whether they hear or refuse to hear, they will know that there has been a prophet among them.

The key word "send" stands out. This sending is to the "rebellious" vassal people. There Ezekiel has to appear as an official ambassador: "Thus has so and so spoken" is the formula with which a diplomat introduces his embassy. The possibility of the failure of the prophet's mission is also taken into account. Even in this case, the sending of the ambassador has its meaning: the vassal has been warned. God is in the right, if he now takes measures against rebellious Israel. There is no doubt that Ezekiel understood his task from the time of his vocation entirely within the framework of the covenant. This task is to bring into effect in Israel, in the name of God, the covenant law of God.

This also can be seen clearly from the content and form of the message which he proclaims. He is naturally acquainted with many different techniques of preaching. But very often he alludes by paraphrase to texts from the covenant cult, which was known to his audience. This is the case, for example, in a judgment speech which is attached to one of the first groups of symbolic actions, Ezekiel 5:5–17. The punishments which Ezekiel threatens there derive almost verbally from an early form of the blessing and cursing text which now concludes the Law of Holiness in the present Pentateuch (Lev 26). The real force of the argument of the speech lies in these allusions. To express the matter in abstract terms, Ezekiel is saying: You have not kept the law of the covenant, so now the covenant curses associated with this covenant law will fall upon you.

But how does Ezekiel understand the law in such contexts? Is his conception of it a Pauline one, that of a divine will forcing men into sin? We must affirm once again, in the case of Ezekiel, the presence of a non-Pauline view of the law. The law is always the will of God, preceded by the grace of God. The judgment speech in Ezekiel 5:5–17 begins:

> Jerusalem: I have set her in the center of the nations, with countries round about her . . .

Thus Yahweh has made Jerusalem the center of the world. It is from this act of grace that Yahweh's demands upon his holy city Jerusalem first derive. There is no divine demand, which was planned from the first on the basis of sin, to lead to sin. Instead, Ezekiel also sees the law as now working, in the apostasy of Israel and the punishment which follows, against the purpose which it was intended to have by God. Thus Ezekiel, too — and probably all the prophets — accepts the general position of the Israelite theology of the covenant, and holds a view in which the evaluation of the significance of the law in the history of salvation is not in accord with that of Paul.

## Conclusion

This overwhelming consensus on the part of the Old Testament against Paul raises a problem for us. The Old Testament regards itself as belonging within the realm of grace. Paul himself naturally accepts this view, in that he claims "for faith," Abraham and everything which possesses the nature of promise, and thus, by relating it directly to Christ, separates it from the Old Testament. But the Old Testament avoids such a break, at least in the great bulk of its main statements, which we have been examining. It places the law with far less concern than Paul within the context of grace.

One may ask whether Paul perhaps may have spoken in so negative a fashion of the Mosaic law, because the assumption with which he started was that any faith, grace, or life which existed in Israel before Christ must from the very first be seen in a different context, on the line leading from Abraham to Christ. By doing this, he abstracted from the law its positive possibility, leaving only this demonic force, impelling toward sin.

If this is the case, then it virtually depends only on one's starting point whether one's judgment upon the law is that of Paul, or genuinely that of the Old Testament. Or one might say that it is a question of the concepts one uses. In this case, it would perhaps be possible to maintain both modes of thought simultaneously: that of the Old Testament, which sees grace and the law as unity, a unity which is always imperiled, and that of Paul, which concentrates everything positive in the grace of Abraham and everything negative in its concept of the law.

Perhaps one could even follow the typical method of Old Testament thought and formulate a New Testament statement which would give Christ his unique eschatological dignity by contrast with all earlier ways of salvation written by God. If this were done, then Paul would be deprived of the monopoly which permits him alone to give a competent statement concerning the relationship between the two testaments. But perhaps this has been done already in other New Testament writings — if not in other Pauline epistles apart from Romans and Galatians.

# CHAPTER SEVEN

# FREEDOM AND REPETITION

*On the Understanding of History in the Old Testament*
The Old Testament does not possess any specific word for what
we call "history." Nevertheless, if one seeks to define the understanding of history in the Old Testament, one probably can not
avoid setting out the whole theology of the Old Testament.
Lengthy sections of the two-volume *Theology of the Old Testament* by Gerhard von Rad contain virtually nothing but the
theology of history, so intensively is the Old Testament concerned
with history at every period and in all its utterances. It will constantly be necessary to define closely the theme of the following
discussion of the understanding of history in the Old Testament.
This is the reason for our title, "Freedom and Repetition," which
is intended to specify the questions we shall ask. What is the
meaning of this expression?

## *Dynamic and Static Understanding of*
*History at the Present Day*
At the present moment of history, all mankind is growing
closer together. This movement has never been so rapid. Despite
all the tension, distress and misery on earth, the world is moving
at an ever-increasing rate toward unity. Through the spread of
technology and better organization, it is approaching a new form
of existence common to the whole of mankind, something which

is sensed rather than clearly perceived, but is approaching in-eluctably. Even the national peculiarities of old and young nations can be only regarded as the offshoots of an irresistible world proc-ess — at least in anticipation. Not only does this process have its source as a matter of fact in the West, but its intellectual sub-stance is determined by the West. Much more is taking place than a mere reorganization of the distribution of goods or the extension of the possibilities of communication. Intellectual up-heavals are in progress. In particular, humanity is being brought into a new relationship to history. It is a secondary matter in this regard whether the prevailing view is the Marxist, the Christian, or the liberal-postivist version of what the West has to offer.

In any case the ancient civilized nations of Africa and Asia, and above all small archaic and primitive groups, are wrenched out of the static situation which has provided their environment, and drawn into a dynamic movement of human life which was hitherto completely alien to them. Everything is in motion toward the future.

We must not evaluate this passage to a dynamic state on the part of hitherto static groups of human beings, in a naïve Euro-pean fashion, as a passage from the childhood stage of humanity to a condition of intellectual maturity, or as a step from imper-fection toward perfection. Instead, this static mode of existence, out of which we are now forcing the greater part of humanity, should be regarded in the first instance as a pure phenomenon, before any evaluation is made, and it should be conceded, at least at first, that perhaps it may be as adult and complete an attitude to history as our historical dynamism. In fact, could not the re-verse be the case, that our modern preoccupation with history is nothing more than a fever which must possess the body of humanity for several centuries, only to pass away once again, and give place to a new static stage in a reconstituted world?

Do we know that progress will go on forever? Is it not possible that one day the limits of natural science may be reached, the reservoir of technology exhausted, and the passion for novelty abated. True, if this is ever to happen, there is still an immense distance to go before it does. But we cannot rule out the possibility altogether. Perhaps the arrival of this condition is heralded by the new problems which our time has to face, such as that of what man is to do with the leisure gained by rationalization. In any case, we ought not to dismiss as immature, childish and primitive nations, worlds and civilizations which do not see the meaning of existence in the progress of history, but rather in withdrawing from history in a static mode of existence.

There are two simple basic attitudes to history which are possible. They are to the same extent mature human choices, even though one may threaten to consume the other for a time. Our watchword is "freedom." Our gaze is set upon the future. Constantly creating novelties, we look for everything from the forward movement of time. Archaic societies and the great classical civilizations suffered from the passage of time. They sought permanence beyond the assaults of history. Thus they overcame its constant motion through "repetition." They brought back to the surface what was sinking to oblivion in the stream of time. Their conscious achievement consists of diverting for the human consciousness the straight line of time into a circle, in which the same thing recurs, the present moment is preserved, and the terror of the transistory is assuaged.

We are carried along by time. We guide it and fill it. Others turn away from it, fleeing into rites which constantly repeat themselves and lift men up into the pure and elemental forms of the mythical interpretation of existence. We find our meaning in history. Others withdraw from history, in order to find their meaning in a primal age, lying outside history, but accessible in rites to men who are subject to time. Thus "freedom and repetition," the theme of the study that follows, places us in a tension between two diametrically opposed attitudes to history, which in our present world are in fruitful conflict; and despite the momentary advantage of one, it is not impossible that perhaps the other may have the greater power of endurance, just as it is the older, the source from which our confidence in a dynamic history sprang at a very very late hour in the life of mankind.

It is also true that however secular and anti-Christian the modern understanding of history often may seem to be at present, in its origin and development it is wholly determined by the Judaeo-Christian religion of revelation. Anyone who seeks to understand this attitude toward history must attempt to understand Christianity. Anyone who seeks its origins must concern himself with the Old Testament. For it is there that it began. It is there, as far as we can see at the present day, that it first resisted the cyclical conception, the view that it was possible to stand still in the stream of time, the rite which renewed the world and the mythology of creation which underlay everything. Anyone who attempts to understand and interpret what is going on at present at a very profound level — no longer, perhaps, in Europe, but within humanity as a whole — will find that what is reflected in the Old Testament is indispensable to them.

## The Question to Be Posed

That is why the theme of our study is so important. How did this consciousness of history, which is now in the process of gaining acceptance throughout the whole world, begin? Did it inevitably possess, we shall go on to ask, in its first origins as in its realizations, the monstrous urge to destruction which it now displays, or did it manifest in its origins possibilities of reconciliation and synthesis which we must regain?

If these questions are to provide the basis of the study that follows, then we must show that in ancient Israel a completely new attitude toward history appeared, and we must also show how this came about. The situation is not as simple as it is often represented to be, even by Gerhard von Rad. We must first reconstruct the background with which Israel must be contrasted. What was the attitude of the ancient East toward history?

## The Attitude Toward History in the Ancient Near East

We must first set aside a frequent misunderstanding. A cyclical understanding of history does not mean that the group of people concerned had a fundamentally different experience of time from ours. Ancient man experienced the same flow of time as we do. The moment crumbles away, drawing back into the *No Longer* of the past, while new moments are constantly built up from the

*Not Yet* of the future. It is even perfectly possible to conceive objectively of a "line of time," and if in many cases this is not extended very far into the past and the future, this is due to accidental circumstances. For the most part, there is not much material in the form of historical recollection available. Nevertheless, the line of time may in some cases, in an antiquity which is still wholly unhistorical, be extended to an astonishing length.

The State Museum in Berlin possesses from Egypt the genealogy of a family of priests at Memphis, embracing sixty generations and extending continuously over some thirteen hundred years. How many noble houses in Europe can show the same? The basic linear experience of time can be seen represented in wholly visual terms in a monument from the fifth or sixth dynasty of Egypt (approximately 2500 B.C.), in the "Annals of the Old Kingdom," known as the Palermo Stone. There, a right angle is drawn for each year of the kings from the first dynasty on, and in the right angle the events of the year are inscribed; the right angles are then built up one upon the other. In the Mesopotamian region the linear experience of time is given a most powerful symbolic expression in the "Sumerian king list," which probably comes from the twenty-third century B.C. It sets out a line of kings which descends continuously from the moment when "the monarchy descended from heaven." Although in fact many of these kings ruled simultaneously in different Mesopotamian city states, they are now all placed upon a single line of time.

Thus it is very improbable that ancient man was unable to conceive of time as a linear succession of situations running in a single direction. Rather, that is the general assumption, common to all mankind, which underlies different attitudes, and from which they differ only later. For this is perfectly possible. For example, of great immediate importance is the direction in which a person in a given culture normally looks, toward the past or toward the future. Astonishing light is cast on this by language. For example, for those speaking modern European languages, the future is in front and the past is behind. "Now I have that behind me," someone will say after taking an examination. The yearly statement of a company says, "We look forward to the future with confidence." By contrast, the Hebrew word for "future," exactly translated, means "what lies behind," while the word for the "distant past" is "what lies in front." The speaker is looking in the direction of the past.

These insignificant lexicographical observations in themselves reveal completely different emphases and evaluations within the same general human experience of time. But it would be a methodological error to derive from observations of this kind on the Hebrew language any conclusions about the historical understanding, in the first millennium B.C., of the Israelites who spoke this Hebrew language. The Hebrew language is older. We cannot exclude the possibility that the attitude toward time of the Israelites whom we know from history was different from what is expressed in their language. But at least the observation we have mentioned shows how the common experience of humanity, of standing in the stream of time, can be differently interpreted with regard to its significance and structure.

We must also note that even a positive interest in the past does not of itself imply a definite understanding of history in the sense of the questions we propose. For example, in Egypt there was a great concern to preserve the memory of individual events and to hand them down to posterity, although the view of history there rested unambiguously upon the idea of the constantly renewed repetition of time, with the reigns of the Pharaohs following each other as manifestations of the act by which the world was created. Similarly, an interest in the past can be found very early in Mesopotamia, and was expressed in different literary forms. Before the Israelites, the greatest precision in the presentation of the long sequences of historical events is to be found in the Hittite annals, and in the historical parts of Hittite state treaties from the second millennium B.C.

But an interest in the past at this time necessarily accompanies a certain level of culture and civilization. It does not necessarily imply a quite specific interpretative understanding of the experience of time. But it is this alone with which we are concerned in the present study. The understanding of time in the ancient Near East before and around Israel was essentially unhistorical and cyclical. The cities, the states and also individual men lived in the rhythm of the cult. The festivals, and above all, apparently, the new year festival, in which the world passed away and was built up again, provided the structure of their consciousness. It was in the festivals that one could obtain true life, lifted up above time. Everything else received its power from this. This was true of the ancient Sumerian rites of the sacred marriage, as well as of the Babylonian *akitu* festival or the Canaanite fertility rites, which are not known to us in detail, but which represented a constant temptation to Israel, and were therefore a constant challenge to the pastoral concern of the prophets.

There is no point here in going in detail into the infinitely varied world of the rites of the ancient Near East, but it is perhaps worth emphasizing that the king, who to us at the present day represents the incarnation of political life and therefore of what is bound up with history, who was above all else the central figure of the ritual. Whereas it may have been the acts of government and the military activity of the ruler which were in fact of decisive importance, what mattered to the consciousness of the time was that as the essence and symbol of his whole people, he duly carried out the ritual and therefore increased the life force within the sphere to which his radiance extended. In fact, for example, it was possible for the Hittite emperor Mursilis II (fourteenth century B.C.), who was constantly forced to undertake military campaigns by external threats, to allow himself to be replaced by a deputy in the supreme command, because as the king he was detained in the capital by the rites.

Consequently, however violent the wars which took place in this world, and however violent the cultural upheavals which took place, only the outer fringes of the consciousness were affected, because the center of human consciousness was completely filled by the mythical beings with which a timeless link was forged by the constantly repeated rite. Within the rite, man and the nation found security from the storms and oppressions of history. And ancient man sought this security, whereas we often seem to long for insecurity.

Naturally, insecurity was an ever present menace, and with the rise of high civilizations, the growth of political systems, and the increase in the violence and unpredictability of the vicissitudes of fate, man was compelled to reflect upon history. We can give a brief outline here of the two main directions which this reflection seems to have taken in the region of Mesopotamia and Asia Minor.

One can be seen in its earliest form in what are known as lists of omens. They belong to the realm of the Mesopotamian technique of divination, which was practiced above all by the inspection of the liver of sacrificed sheep. Its basic assumption was the idea that every moment of time represents a kind of total situation in which every detail is related to every other. There is only a finite, albeit relatively large number of such total sets of related circumstances in the world. Former sets of related circumstances can recur at any time, although it is quite impossible to calculate their sequence. If one succeeded in defining a given world situation by certain accessible criteria, then it can be recognized and taken into account in one's actions. If one makes the further assumption that the form of the liver of a sacrificed animal bears a fixed relation to the total set of related circumstances in the world at a moment of the sacrifice, then one can build upon it an exact science of the interpretation of omens. Today, naturally, we no longer accept this assumption as correct. But once one accepts this as a hypothesis, it is clear that the Babylonian science of augury could work on principle in the same way as our weather forecasts.

In the course of time, experiences concerning the different sets of related circumstances were gathered, and at any particular moment it was possible to draw conclusions from the form of the liver about the present situation and its further development. As a consequence, the earlier world situations, together with the forms of the liver which occurred at that time, were gathered into the so-called lists of omens. The form these took was roughly: "If the liver has such and such a form ( a detailed description of the form of the liver is given), this is an omen of the king of

Apishal, whom Naramsin captured, when he tried to break through the wall of his city." For it was known that at that time the liver had taken that particular form.

It is presumably clear how the examination of omens functioned. What we are now interested in is the understanding of history expressed in it. Behind it lies the experience that the actual course of history is irrational, and does not automatically follow the cyclical order of the festivals. Rather, there were times of fortune and misfortune, which follow in an incalculable sequence. But with the help of the knowledge of omens, one can to some extent come to terms with it. When unfavorable sets of circumstances exist, then one avoids dangerous enterprises, but if favorable sets of circumstances arise, then one makes use of them. Perhaps one might change the circumstances through magic and prayers of conjuration. A reflection is being made upon history, and — and this is where it derives its importance — history is not felt to be really the sphere of the plans and self-realization of man, but rather as an interference coming from outside, against which one has to defend oneself by scientific knowledge. The whole system of omens is a derivative of the basic cyclical attitude which is not interested in history. It does not bring man into a new positive relationship to history, even though in some of the lists of omens a great deal of material containing historical experience is assembled.

The same is true of another kind of historical formula, which appears to come from the realm of what is known as "wisdom." Whereas the idea underlying the list of omens is still that of an irrational succession of different periods of fortune and misfortune, the ancient Near Eastern philosophy which we know as "wisdom" arrived by generalizing upon many individual observations at the conviction that there was a fundamental link between human actions and their outcome. Thus history no longer was regarded as mere arbitrary succession, but as a series of consequences. This is perhaps most clearly reflected in what is known as the "Weidner Chronicle." In it the history of Mesopotamia from the time of the flood is recounted. In practice, it argues that every misfortune which has come about in history has been the result of a transgression of a ruling king against the cult in the temple of Marduk in Babylon. This conception of history is also characteristic of the Hittite historical accounts, and can be seen particularly clearly in the famous "plague prayers" of Mursilis.

Despite a quite astonishing precision in the attention paid to the arbitrary events of history, here, too, history is taken seriously only insofar as it upsets the normal condition of good fortune. The cause of the disturbance is even located for the most part in the cultic transgressions of man, and especially of the king. If the cult had been properly carried out, and furthermore — an addition made by the Hittites — all treaty obligations had been maintained, then it would not have been necessary to worry about the vicissitudes of history. Thus here, too, we do not find a full acceptance of history, but only a concern for knowledge within a total understanding which is quite uninterested in the course of history as such. It is at this point that a different view is adopted in Israel.

## The New Attitude Toward History in Israel

In Israel history is introduced in the rites, that is, in the strictly religious sphere. We can see this clearly from a text in the Book of Deuteronomy, the law concerning the offering of the first fruits from the annual harvest (Dt 26:1–11). The first fruits are brought into the sanctuary; the priest places them before the altar, and then the following confession of faith is uttered:

> "A wandering Aramean was my father; and he went down into Egypt and sojourned there, few in number; and there he became a nation, great, mighty, and populous. And the Egyptians treated us harshly, and afflicted us, and laid upon us hard bondage. Then we cried to Yahweh the God of our fathers, and Yahweh heard our voice, and saw our affliction, our toil, and our oppression; and Yahweh brought us out of Egypt with a mighty hand and an outstretched arm, with great terror, with signs and wonders; and he brought us into this place and gave us this land, a land flowing with milk and honey. And behold, now I bring the first of the fruit of the ground, which thou, O Yahweh, hast given me" (Dt 26:6–10).

As children of an age which breathes the breath of atheism, we are tempted to be surprised that here a deity is presented as the force shaping history. But there is nothing exceptional in this. It is not a new idea, in the light of all the comparable non-Israelite texts in the ancient Near East. Although we have not yet · mentioned this, it was naturally accepted, as in the framework of every other ancient Near Eastern attitude to history, that everything which took place in the historical sphere was determined by the divine sphere. Naturally, all the sets of related circumstances which can be recognized by omens are brought about by gods. Naturally, the gods guarantee the link between actions and their outcome, as for example, when the omission of the sacrifice by the king brings a period of misfortune for the nation. Thus that the leading of Israel out of Egypt and into the promised land should be professed to be an act of Yahweh is not surprising, however much it may shock our historical thought, impregnated by unbelief as it is.

What is new is the weight which this statement concerning divine action in history derives from the context in which it stands.

The law is dealing with the harvest festival. Perhaps it refers to one of the three feasts at which all Israel assembled. In that case, it would be the Feast of Weeks, which corresponds to our Pentecost. In any case, the subject of the festival is the fruit of the land. Thus we are dealing with something closely related to the Canaanite festivals which celebrated, in the fertility of the land, renewed every year, the cyclical mystery of the life force. It is at this very point, where Eastern tradition introduced, as the legend underlying the feast, myths of creation or of the resurrection of the fertility god imprisoned in the underworld, that Israel introduced an historical narrative. In the festival Israel did not reach out of the passing stream of time into the primal age of ideal archetypes, which could be located anywhere or nowhere, but went back a few decades, and later a few centuries along the line of time, remaining within history and basing the festival upon historical events. Nothing like this previously had been done with history. Its arbitrary content had never before served to give a meaning to existence. In Israel this is something new.

The new weight placed upon history can be demonstrated from two phenomena which at first seem to be contradictory: the interest in history in Israel which increased rapidly at an early period, and the mythologizing of history.

Even though, as we have already explained, there existed in the ancient Near East, long before the time of Israel, and expressed in the most diverse literary categories, catalogs of historical facts and accounts of history in the form of general summaries, these remained a marginal type of literary activity, or served strictly practical purposes. There was never anything which we could call in our modern sense "history writing." By contrast, in Israel it is evident that a concern with what had happened in the past came to be a central concern of writers at an early stage. No people in the ancient Near East concerned itself so intensively with this history as Israel. Moreover, Israel very rapidly, only two centuries after the period of the foundation, reached a level of history writing which led Eduard Meyer, the great historian of antiquity, to the judgment that true historical literature (in our modern sense) began in Israel. The period of David and Solomon already was able to produce accounts of a single period as significant as the "history of the succession to the throne of David," and a universal history without previous parallels, the work of the "Yahwist." In these, the presentation of individual figures and events frequently attained a complexity and a fullness of reality which no other literature of the ancient world is able to give.

Erich Auerbach has demonstrated this in his book *Mimesis*, using the example of the sacrifice of Isaac. There is no doubt that this power of literary expression on the part of Israel in portraying history derives from the emphasis laid upon historical events in Israel's cult, and therefore in its religious understanding of itself.

The same fact, however, produced simultaneously a phenomenon which to our modern eyes is completely contradictory to the first, that of the mythologizing of history. Precisely because in Israel historical facts took the place which previously had been occupied by myths enacted in the primal age, in reciting and alluding to these historical facts in the cult Israel was now able to give them an appeal to the senses and due emphasis by embellishing them with typical features of the myth of the primal age. Psalm 114 provides an example of this:

> "When Israel went forth from Egypt, the house of Jacob from a people of strange language, Judah became his sanctuary, Israel his dominion. The sea looked and fled, Jordan turned back. The mountains skipped like rams, the hills like lambs. What ails you, O sea, that you flee? O Jordan, that you turn back? O mountains, that you skip like rams? O hills, like lambs? Tremble, O earth, at the presence of the Lord, at the presence of the God of Jacob."

Here the historical content of Israel's confession of faith is adorned with features deriving from the myth of creation, in which the creator confronts chaos, conceived of as a sea, and subjects it to himself by his rebuke. Only when the events of the exodus from Egypt are exalted to the level of events in the primal age, by being represented as a new act of creation on the part of Yahweh, do they obtain the dignity through which they can serve to give meaning to existence. Consequently, we must not be misled by the mythological features which recur in the midst of historical works in Israel. The events distinguished in this fashion are regarded as facts occurring in the normal course of history, and what is added to the historical fact is not legendary fantasy, but a statement of belief expressed in the style of the time: these historical events which happened as they did are the foundation underlying our existential life.

Thus in Israel history for the first time was accorded the significance which it still possesses in our understanding of history at the present day. But our modern understanding of history has a further characteristic: it is directed toward the future. We look for true reality in history, and we do not look for it in the past, but in the future. Our understanding of history is — if it is permissible to make use of this word, with its many ambiguities — eschatological. This eschatological view also goes back to Israel.

It is the achievement of the great prophets. This must not be misunderstood. At a very early stage, Israel looked forward to great historical acts of God in the future. When the Yahwist considers the meaning of the history of Israel to be that the blessing of Abraham will at some time extend to "all the families of the earth," then he is looking to a saving act of God in the future (Gen 12:3); and the same is true at the very beginning of history, where the snake is told that the seed of woman will bruise its head, because it snaps at his heels (Gen 3:15). But such expectations from the future did not in the first instance alter the fact that the true act of salvation on which Israel's faith was based lay in the past. This was the leading of Israel out of Egypt and into the promised land.

Only when, during the period of the kings, and above all at the beginning of the exile in Babylon, the ancient order of salvation was increasingly seen to be inadequate and anticipatory did it come about that Israel's gaze was wholly directed toward the future. Instead of the old covenant, "which I made with their fathers when I took them by the hand to bring them out of the land of Egypt," Jeremiah promises in Chapter 31 a "new," greater future covenant. Deutero-Isaiah says toward the end of the exile: "Behold, the former things have come to pass, and new things I now declare; before they spring forth I tell you of them" (Is 42:9). There is no need to discuss the prophetic proclamation of the future at length here; it is something which is well known. Nevertheless, the result of it was once again to shift the emphasis in the understanding of history. History is important for man, and it possesses this importance as future history.

## Israel's Understanding of History As a Synthesis

Thus in ancient Israel at least the basic principles were created of that attitude to history which is characteristic at the present day of Western man, and probably will soon be that of the whole of mankind. Even though in the meantime the concept has been developed without God, from whom alone history derived its significance in Israel, the structure of the understanding of history nevertheless is the same. We are still living on the basis of the transformations in human consciousness which took place in Israel at the time. In essence, they are having their full effect only at the present day.

There is, however, another question which arises. Was Israel in reality so radically opposed to the cyclical attitude of antiquity to the passage of time as we are today? The answer is that it was not. It can be shown that despite a completely new approach to history and to its "freedom," Israel still retained an awareness of "repetition." We have only to recall that the place in which this history was recited was Israel's cult. It became a festival legend, and took on features of the ancient creation myth.

History remained history, consisting of contingent or arbitrary fact at a definite point along the line of time. But in a paradoxical fashion it also took on the character of the primal age, in which all other ages can participate, if they carry out the rite of the feast. Israel once came out of Egypt, and this was and remained a historical fact. But at the same time each new generation of Israel was able, at every new year in the Passover feast, when the Passover lamb slain at first was slain once again, and eaten in haste as before, to enter itself into the past event and participate in it. Each generation could begin to live anew through this, as though it were now happening for the very first time. The covenant has been made between Israel and its God once for all. But Israel repeatedly assembles. Then the cultic pronounces the words which we read today in Deuteronomy 5:1–3:

> "Hear, O Israel, the stautes and the ordinances which I speak in your hearing this day, and you shall learn them and be careful to do them. Yahweh our God made a covenant with us in Horeb. Not with our fathers did Yahweh make this covenant, but with us, who are all of us here alive this day."

One cannot identify the two diffrent times more closely. The events at the beginning of the history of Israel have taken over the function of the primal age of creation. The arbitrary events of history, without ceasing to be history, have at the same time come to the place of refuge which assists man to free himself from that arbitrary course of history which oppresses him during his life.

As the course of history proceeds, it will never bring what is wholly unknown and incalculable, for Israel knows how its God Yahweh, the creator of heaven and earth and the sole Lord of all history, habitually acts within history.

Consequently, Israel is now able to interpret every period of history on the basis of its primal age, that of the Exodus and the entry into Canaan. In the first place, it now possesses categories in which to understand the past which came before this "primal age." It is possible for Israel to speak even in the case of Abraham of a "covenant" between God and Abraham, or even to go back still further and acknowledge in the case of Noah a "covenant" of God with the whole of mankind. Similarly, the present time can always be understood on the basis of the events in the age of Israel's foundation, and when the prophets bring about the great redirection of attention toward the future, then it is automatic for the great act of salvation by God in the future to receive only names such as "new exodus," "new covenant," "new entry into the promised land," and "new David." The past and the future correspond. This understanding of history is typological. Thus it is in Israel that history was taken seriously for the first time, yet in such a way that besides the principle of "freedom" that of "repetition" was never forgotten.

## An Attempt At an Evaluation

Is the principle of repetition in Israel's understanding of history something of genuine value? Or is it perhaps merely an inconsistency, a sign of inability to accept something radically new into the original attitude toward history without distorting it?

The question must be posed, for at some point we must begin to evaluate the different possible attitudes. The question cannot be answered on the basis of the Old Testament — at least not if as a Christian one derives one's ultimate standard of value from the New Testament. Let us look then at the New Testament. Is the Israelite approach to history, which it was still possible to reconcile with the understanding of history which was that of repetition, so radicalized by the New Testament as to become a completely uncompromising view of history, which affirmed only the continuing passage of time, the constantly changing situation, and a future which is always different from the present? Or does the New Testament maintain the demand for a synthesis between freedom and repetition, such as was created in the Old Testament?

In fact the coming of Christ did not weaken at all, in the first instance, the principle of repetition, but rather that of the historical outlook which is directed toward the future. For in Christ the expectation aroused by the prophets was fulfilled. With Christ the time of salvation has returned; in fact, the unrepeatable and final time of salvation is present. Thus after the coming of Christ, we can really only exist by looking into the past. To use the language of comparative religion, Christ is our primal age. We can do nothing except to realize in the cult what happened "in that time." Thus the expectation of the future created by the prophets is no longer necessary! At the same time, however, we must add a complementary thesis which is also the teaching of New Testament. Christ has not yet come, and remains our future. The parousia of Christ is still before us. There is still a tension which draws us toward the future. The attitude aroused in Israel by the prophets must therefore continue, although their expectation has been fulfilled.

The statement: "In Christ God acted finally in history" and "in Christ God will act finally in history," must both be combined to form the Christian understanding of history. It follows from this that correspondences between different ages remain. It would be to misunderstand the New Testament, to quote it against the principle of repetition.

If this is so, then certainly the completely onesided belief in progress which at the present day dominates the technical civilization of the West, and which as we affirmed at the beginning of this study, is in the process of replacing every other attitude to history among the ancient civilized nations of the world, cannot be regarded as Christian, however much its roots may seem to lie in the Christian revelation, or more precisely in the Old Testament. It is a radical extreme, which has destroyed a synthesis for the sake of one part of it. It seeks only the freedom in the historical process, its forward motion, without any repetition.

It is also clear how this was bound to happen. The synthesis between freedom and repetition in the understanding of history is only possible if God is taken into account. Only the universal presence of the eternity of God overshadowing the constant passage of time makes it possible for an historical contingent moment to possess at the same time the nature of a primal age, capable of being a repeatable, power-providing, meaningful and life-giving underlying form for every human existential life. In fact ultimately only the mystery of Christ, that of being God and man at once, makes this possible. Without this coexistence of time and eternity, the affirmation of history, once one has decided in favor of it, is bound to result in one's being swallowed up by the absolutely unidirectional flow of time. All that then remains is the purely secular eschatology of belief in progress or of Marxism, or else the existentialist retreat into the despair of the present moment, which passes into nothingness as soon as it comes into being.

It must also be added that the way in which the world is dynamically organized toward unity at the present day also could be possible from the point of view of a Christian understanding of history. For it implies both that historical reality is taken seriously and that its goal is set in the future. It has the further advantage of not destroying the world of repetition for the older civilizations, but of raising it into a higher synthesis. It is evident that Christians at present have the task of saving and developing further the basic attitudes of the older civilizations. The course history is now following is tending to deprive them of "repetition" for the sake of "freedom." Why is it not possible to create a structure of the consciousness in which the words "freedom and repetition" both apply? This is the task.

# CHAPTER EIGHT

# MAN FACE TO FACE WITH DEATH

Civilization banishes death to the hospital, hides it behind a barrier of hypodermics, and secretly longs for it in the form of sudden death in a car accident. At the same time, however, it is becoming a central theme in our philosophy. What place did the "philosophy" of Israel, which we know of as "wisdom," find in its thinking for death? To what extent were its counsels for man and for his life determined by the inevitable approach of death?

Thus we shall not be inquiring into conceptions of death and "life after death," although we shall have to mention them. The real object of this study is the attitude of man toward them. The wisdom of the Old Testament does not offer us a single universally held answer to this question. Instead, we shall meet different answers, which stand in a dialectical relationship to each other.

## *Death in the Ancient Experimential Wisdom of Israel*

The ancient collections of proverbs which are preserved in Proverbs 10–31 still belong to the realm of wisdom based on popular experience, which sums up the manifold phenomena of reality by formulating "proverbs." A typical feature of this attitude toward knowledge is its unsystematic character. Every new experience is summarized in as brief a saying as possible; individual fragments of knowledge are listed one after the other, and contradictory experiences are not reconciled, but consciously opposed to one another, in order to attain a comprehension of reality as full and extensive as possible. Thus in this proverbial wisdom, death, and the attitude of man toward death, appear in different lights, and the very diverse theses of the later systematizing wisdom of Israel could basically all appeal to ancient statements of the wisdom which was based on experience.

An assumption so obvious that we shall not discuss it further in itself is the knowledge that life eventually comes to an end. If we seek to know the concepts in which this statement was expressed by the Israelites, we can find them more easily in the Psalms or in the Book of Job than in Proverbs. The concept is one of an existence reduced almost to nothing, without power, voice, life, knowledge or the possibility of action — localized in "Sheol," the underworld. It is the place "whence I shall not return, the land of gloom and deep darkness, the land of gloom and chaos, where light is as darkness" (Job 10:21 f.).

God overwhelms man forever, and he travels thither; God disfigures his countenance and sends him away; "his sons come to honor, and he does not know it; they are brought low, and he perceives it not" (Job 14:20 f.). "My eye will never again see good. The eye of him who sees me will behold me no more; while thy eyes are upon me, I shall be gone. As the cloud fades and vanishes, so he who goes down to Sheol does not come up; he returns no more to his house, nor does his place know him any more" (Job 7:7–10). The existence of the "shades" in Sheol is the negation of everything which we experience as possessing being and value in our earthly existence. This thought, which uses concrete images, must always think in terms of some form of existence, and only attempts to make it as shadowy as possible.

Perhaps one would not be doing justice to Israel if one asserted that these statements concerning the shades in the underworld can be simply interpreted to mean that death is the end of everything, and that man no longer exists in any sense or in any respect. But at least one must interpret them by saying that death is the end of life. Nor is this acknowledged with resentment or a rebellious spirit, but is taken for granted — even when it is the cause of suffering. A given number of years is accorded to man, seventy, or at most eighty, according to Psalm 90:10; or at the very outside, a hundred years, according to Ecclesiasticus 18:9. Man's purpose must be that these years be truly filled with "life," for they are there only once, and then they are past, and "life" is at an end. This is true of all men without exception, whether they are wise or foolish. This is the automatic assumption of the ancient Israelite wisdom, based on experience, whenever it mentions death. With this in mind, not a great deal of fuss is made of death — by contrast to such a passage as Psalm 90, where the person who prays the psalm is cast into agitation and inner distress by the thought of death alone. For the proverbial wisdom, it is simply something that exists. "We must all die, we are like water spilt on the ground, which cannot be gathered up again" — so says the wise woman to King David (2 Sam 14:14).

But the "death" on which the ancient wisdom reflects tends rather to be early, or more precisely, premature death. Why does it exist, and how can it be avoided? These two questions are posed, and they show that premature death was seen as something which was not to be taken for granted, as in the nature of things, but was regarded as something different from normal death at the end of a life which had been fulfilled and was drawing to its end. In the case of premature death, this ancient wisdom sees at work a connection between man's deeds and the results that follow it:

He who pursues evil will die (Pr 11:19).

This is based on concrete observation. Anyone who only desires, but never turns his hand to work, must one day hunger:

The desire of the sluggard kills him,
for his hands refuse to labor (Pr 21:25).

But individual observations of this kind are then generalized into statements of principle concerning "fools":

Fools die for lack of sense (Pr 10:21).

These proverbs show how one can avoid a premature death:

The teaching of the wise is a fountain of life,
that one may avoid the snares of death (Pr 13:14).

The fear of the Lord is the fountain of life,
that one may avoid the snares of death (Pr 14:27).

This realization, also, that one can avoid the threat of death,
rests in the first instance on concrete experience, and the general
statement is a later derivative of this:

A king's wrath is a messenger of death,
and a wise man will appease it (Pr 16:14).

Death and life are in the power of the tongue,
and those who curb it (R.S.V.: "love it") will eat
its fruits (Pr 18:21).

Through wisdom man places as much distance as possible between himself and the underworld:

The wise man's path leads upward to life,
that he may avoid Sheol beneath (Pr 15:24).

In educating the young in wisdom, the threat of an early death
seems to have formed an important theme:

He who hates reproof will die (Pr 15:10).

Do not withhold discipline from a child;
if you beat him with a rod, he will not die.
If you beat him with the rod
you will save his life from Sheol (Pr 23:13 f.).

Discipline your son while there is hope;
do not set your heart on his destruction (Pr 19:18).

In all these passages, death is not in fact specifically characterized as premature death, but is evidently meant as such. The
best commentary on these texts is perhaps the second speech of
Zophar, a typical representative of the older wisdom, in the Book
of Job. There he says of the wicked:

His bones are full of youthful vigor,
but it will lie down with him in the dust (Job 20:11).

Thus the proverbial wisdom fears only this premature death,
but knows whence it comes, and knows also how it can be
avoided.

But as it is the genuine wisdom of experience, it does not
harden into a system. It places side by side with the statements

quoted above, other statements which call into question their self-assurance.

Even a wise man can suffer an early death, as a proverb which is recorded twice affirms with astonishment:

> There is a way which seems right to a man,
> but its end is the way to death (Pr 14:12; 16:25).

Finally, it is not man but God who decides who is subject to death. This is affirmed by the following proverb, in which one must note that the "pit" can be another word for the "underworld":

> The mouth of a loose woman is a deep pit;
> he with whom the Lord is angry will fall into it (Pr 22:14).

Statements such as these show the open-mindedness of the ancient wisdom of experience. It was thereby able to provide a starting point for quite different modes of philosophical encounter with death, of which we shall only examine the most important here.

### Death in the Systematic Wisdom Based on the Concept of the Covenant

We refer here to the nine chapters which — probably in the post-exilic period — were placed before the ancient collections of proverbs in the Book of Proverbs as a kind of interpretative key, and in which the thought of Deuteronomy in particular can be seen to be the formative influence. Here the idea of the connection between foolishness and death is worked out in a systematic way, while the death which threatens man is not merely seen as premature death, but also, in a stronger sense than before, as the sphere of death already surrounding even the sinner who in the biological sense is still alive.

According to Proverb 1–9 man stands at the parting of the ways. He hears the call of wisdom and the call of foolishness, and must decide between them. The way of wisdom leads to life, and the way of foolishness to death. Thus death is not the end of every way, but is the fate of the fool. It is only one of two possibilities open to man. Man can, and ought to avoid it. Let us look at this view more closely.

The "call of wisdom" ends with the promise of "life":

> Wisdom has built her house,
> she has set up her seven pillars.
> She has slaughtered her beasts,
> she has mixed her wine,
> she has also set her table.
> She has sent out her maids to call
> from the highest places in the town,
> "Whoever is simple, let him turn in here!"
> To him who is without sense she says,
> "Come, eat of my bread
> and drink of the wine I have mixed.
> Leave simpleness, and live,
> and walk in the way of insight" (Pr 9:1–6).

Wisdom promises life. Foolishness is deceitful, and naturally, therefore, says nothing of the death to which it leads. But a corresponding passage comments upon its call:

> Foolishness lusts for seduction
> and knows no shame.
> (R.S.V.: 'A foolish woman is noisy;
> she is wanton and knows no shame').
> She sits at the door of her house,
> she takes a seat on the high places of the town,
> calling to those who pass by,
> who are going straight on their way,
> "Whoever is simple, let him turn in here!"
> And to him who is without sense she says,
> "Stolen water is sweet,
> and bread eaten in secret is pleasant."
> But he does not know that the dead are there,
> that her guests are in the depths of Sheol (Pr 9:13–18).

Anyone who partakes of the banquet of foolishness, therefore, is already living the life of one of the shades. He is already in the realm of nothingness. Since "foolishness" in Proverb 1–9 is presented in general in the form of a "strange woman" who seeks to seduce a young man, statements concerning the "strange woman" should also be taken into account:

Many a victim has she laid low;
yea, all her slain are a mighty host.
Her house is the way to Sheol,
going down to the chambers of death (Pr 7:26 f.).

Her house sinks down to death,
and her paths to the shades;
none who go to her come back
nor do they regain the paths of life (Pr 2:18 f.).

Thus death is already there, as soon as one gets involved with foolishness, even though in the bodily sense one is still among the living. One enters into this realm, sinks down into it, and can no longer find the way out. Death is presented as a distinct domain.

Naturally, the old idea of the full length of life and the possibility of its being cut off is still present. Otherwise, the promise of life which this wisdom makes could not have, as it does in many passages, the character of a promise that the biological span of life will be lengthened, as in Proverbs 9:11:

For by me your days will be multiplied,
and years will be added to your life.

Nevertheless, the idea of life and death as two distinct spheres is now the most prominent. Even before man succumbs to a premature death, he may be surrounded by the darkness which is typical of the underworld, and the early age at which death overtakes him is only one element among several which characterize the concept of "death" in this mode of thought:

But the path of the righteous is like the light of dawn,
which shines brighter and brighter until full day.
The way of the wicked is like deep darkness;
they do not know over what they stumble (Pr 4:18 f.).

In this concept of death as a distinct domain can be seen the influence of cultic thought, and in particular that of the covenant cults, upon these chapters. The psalms which beg for deliverance from death, or give thanks for it, often refer to a reality which was present although the person praying was still alive — for example Psalm 18:5 f.:

> The cords of death encompassed me,
> the torrents of perdition assailed me;
> the cords of Sheol entangled me,
> the snares of death confronted me.

In Deuteronomy 30:15–19 we read:

> See, I have set before you this day life and good, death
> and evil . . . I have set before you life and death, bless-
> ing and curse; therefore choose life, that you and your
> descendants may live.

The equivalence of death, misfortune and the curse is clearly recognizable here. The concrete conceptions associated with it can be seen in Deuteronomy 28:16–68, where the cultic curse is given in full. The death with which Israel is threatened in the covenant cult, if the covenant is broken, begins with plagues, confusion and frustration in this life, and physical destruction is only the final culmination of it.

For example, in the Yahwist story of Paradise and the fall we find once again this conception of "death" drawn from the worship of the covenant. When this is realized, the apparent contradiction disappears between the threat of death on the day when the commandment is transgressed, and the fact that the fathers of the race do not die in the biological sense after their sin, but are only driven out of Paradise, where the tree of life stands (Gen 2:17 and 3:23 f.). According to Proverbs 2:22, "death" can begin when a person is driven out of his land. For there, in a context which could equally well speak of death, we read:

> But the wicked will be cut off from the land,
> and the treacherous will be rooted out of it.

On the other hand, wisdom promises man that he can once again gain the tree of life, if he listens to her voice:

> Long life is in her right hand;
> in her left hand are riches and honor.
> Her ways are ways of pleasantness,
> and all her paths are peace.
> She is a tree of life to those who lay hold of her;
> those who hold her fast are called happy (Pr 3:16–18).

Thus the concepts of death and life in the Paradise story undoubtedly are very close to those of Proverbs 1–9. Their common
roots lie in the concept of life and death in the cult.

The text of Proverbs 3:16–18 also contains a concrete account
of what "life" is. It includes length of days (that is, the full
length of life possible for man), riches, honor, peace, and happiness. All this sounds very much of this world, and so it is. It
is in this world, and not in some other world outside it, in which
"life" lies. At the same time all these things have a deeper dimension which provides the real reason why they go to form
"life." It is they alone which bring man into harmony with
God's ordinance of creation. Consequently, the text we have
quoted continues:

> Yahweh by wisdom founded the earth;
> by understanding he established the heavens;
> by his knowledge the deeps broke forth,
> and the clouds dropped down the dew.
> My son, keep sound wisdom and discretion;
> let them not escape from your sight.
> And they will be life for your soul
> and adornment for your neck (Pr 3:19–22).

Thus by following the call of wisdom, one finds one's place in
the ordinance of creation, the ordinance which proceeds from
God — and therefore one is in the domain of life. In accordance
with this, "death" in its profoundest sense is existence remote
from God and his ordinance of creation. Such an existence turns
into nothingness. But one can escape death by choosing the path
of wisdom. Then one is in the domain of life.

This is sufficient to show what is said of death by the systematization of the older wisdom in Proverbs 1–9. It has taken an
aspect which was already in the foreground in the older wisdom,
but was there relativized by contradictory statements, and makes
it completely dominant, going on to give it a more profound dimension through the concept of death as a separate domain. This
systematization was felt to be legitimized by a conscious link with
the cultic traditions of Israel. In this system, death undoubtedly
plays an important part, and is in fact one of the key concepts.

But it is a derivative concept of death, not the total, real and inexorable death which is first and foremost a biological death, and which no man can escape. By sublimating the concept of death, these chapters succeed in limiting it to the realm of sinners, so giving rise to the idea that by particular human actions one can escape death.

It would be unjust perhaps to suggest that real death is thereby consciously or unconsciously excluded from the thought of these chapters. From the start, their attention is directed toward what is possible for man within this life, and no interest is taken in what lies beyond that limit. We must bear in mind that it is possible for man to be concerned with this world alone, and that this possibility can even be a religious one. Almost the whole of the Old Testament presents this possibility alone, and one cannot ever have a genuine encounter with the Old Testament if one regards it on this account as immature ("a revelation which is not yet fully developed"), or as following a false direction ("an inadequate knowledge of the next world"). But of course one must ask whether the Old Testament does not also bear witness to a mode of thought which experiences death in its original biological form as a genuine limit to life, and as a reality which is a genuine offense to this thought.

### Death in the Thought of Qoheleth

Death as the firm limit imposed upon human existence, cutting it off from the infinitely greater potentiality of the progress of time, forms the framework at the beginning and the end of the Book of Qoheleth (= The Preacher = Ecclesiastes). Qoheleth begins by invoking the coming and going of the generations against the background, the stage formed by the solid earth which continually remains:

> A generation goes, and a generation comes,
> but the earth remains for ever (Ec 1:4).

At the end, in his great poem on youth, age and death, he describes the death of man who has grown old, though it is spring-time, when nature, which has also grown old, is once again young and full of life. He goes on to invoke death in images:

. . . the almond tree blossoms,
the grasshopper multiplies,
the caper bears fruit;
(R.S.V.: "the grasshopper drags itself along
and desire fails");
but (R.S.V.: "because") man goes to his eternal home,
and the mourners go about the streets;
when the silver cord is snapped,
the golden bowl is broken,
the pitcher is broken at the fountain,
the wheel broken at the cistern,
and the dust returns to the earth as it was,
and the spirit returns to God who gave it (Ec 12:5–7).

The strange glittering light with which the language used surrounds death here is that which illuminates the whole book. The understanding dissects the problem and never rests until all deceits and half-measures are destroyed, and yet everything is shot through not merely with melancholy, but also with a modest, yet never-failing delight in the happiness which is nevertheless given to man. Qoheleth seeks to guide man into a joyful existence before the face of death, which he never forgets:

Life is sweet,
and it is pleasant for the eyes to behold the sun.
For if a man lives many years,
let him rejoice in them all;
but let him remember that the days of darkness
will be many (Ec 11:7).

How does Qoheleth set about bringing his reader to the point where he remembers the dark days of death?

Qoheleth begins by establishing a starting point which avoids any accusations that he may have introduced a concealed pessimism at the very beginning of his argument, by placing too little value on man's capabilities. He invites the reader to share in an experiment, which begins by looking for the very greatest things of which man is capable. Consequently, he throws off his disguise. He does not present himself to the reader as a teacher of wisdom, who may be a poor man, but:

I the Preacher have been king over Israel in Jerusalem
(Ec 1:12).

He is not necessarily Solomon, the type of the wise and happy man, but he is a man like Solomon. And now the experiment begins. The king, the highest position man can achieve, applies his education, his knowledge, his ability, his power and his wisdom to prepare for himself as much happiness as possible. Thus he seeks to find out:

What was good for the sons of men to do under heaven during the few days of their life (Ec 2:3).

Qoheleth describes how the *homo faber* can transform the world to obtain his own happiness:

I made great works:
I built houses
and planted vineyards for myself;
I made myself gardens and parks,
and planted in them all kinds of fruit trees.
I made myself pools
from which to water the forest of growing trees.
I bought male and female slaves,
and had slaves who were born in my house;
I had also great possessions of herds and flocks,
more than any who had been before me in Jerusalem.
I also gathered for myself silver and gold,
and the treasure of kings and provinces;
I got singers, both men and women,
and many concubines, man's delight.
So I became great and surpassed all that was before me
in Jerusalem;
also my wisdom remained with me.
And whatever my eyes desired I did not keep from them;
I kept my heart from no pleasure (Ec 2:4–10).

Thus Qoheleth, who is guiding the reader toward the thought of death, does not speak of the sinner, but of the wise man. He picks out the finest example of the wise man, the man who belongs to the domain of life not merely by following the moral demands of wisdom, but who also, by using another aspect of wisdom education, that of practical knowledge and technology, can make this domain of life even more intensive, making it the place of unlimited happiness and unlimited joy here upon earth. In conclusion Qoheleth affirms that it is possible for something like this to be given to man, as his "reward" from fate:

> My heart found pleasure in all my toil,
> And this was my reward for all my toil (Ec 2:10).

With this he had laid down the starting point of his argument. Qoheleth did not make his starting point too low, and did not secretly introduce a pessimistic conclusion into his premise.

He continues to give an anticipation of the dismaying conclusion of the line of thought which he is about the pursue:

> Then I considered all that my hands had done, and the toil I had spent in doing it, and behold, all was vanity and a striving after wind, and there was nothing to be gained under the sun (Ec 2:11).

How does his thought lead him to this surprising conclusion? Qoheleth now sets out his argument more precisely. His question is whether, as is asserted, the wise man really possesses life and the fool death:

> So I turn to consider the wisdom and madness and folly . . . then I saw (on the one hand): that wisdom excels folly as light excels darkness:
> > The wise man has his eyes in his head,
> > but the fool walks in darkness.
>
> And yet I perceived that (on the other hand):
> > one fate comes to all of them.
> Then I said to myself, "What befalls the fool will befall me also;
> Why then have I been so very wise?"
> And I said to myself that this also is vanity (Ec 2:12–15).

Thus Qoheleth acknowledges the doctrine that in this life the fool is surrounded by the darkness which other types of wisdom literature already had termed "death"; but he contrasts with this the further fact that true death takes all men. And this casts doubt for him on the significance of being wise. Here he has to face an objection from the thought of the ancient Near East. Does not the wise man still endure, even though he dies — that is, in the reputation that remains after him? Qoheleth sweeps this objection scornfully and imperiously to one side. He already has refuted the idea of eternal honor in his introductory poem in 1:11.

> For of the wise man as of the fool there is no enduring remembrance, seeing that in the days to come all will have been long forgotten (Ec 2:16).

Thus even the wise man must face the end as a bitter reality. Qoheleth seizes upon the consequences of this for his basic attitude. In the face of the consideration of death he has so far maintained the basic attitude of resolution before the world and the will to dominate. Now he concludes that hatred of life is the appropriate attitude:

> How the wise man dies just like a fool! So I hated life, because what is done under the sun was grievous to me; for all is vanity and a striving after wind (Ec 2:16 f.).

Qoheleth repeats his statement that he hates life, by introducing a new aspect into his consideration. Whereas he had previously directed his attention toward the wise man, who comes to an end, he now turns to the work of the wise man, which slips out of his hands. Others take it up, and there is no way of determining what they will make of it:

> I hated all my toil in which I had toiled under the sun, seeing that I must leave it to the man who will come after me; and who knows whether he will be a wise man or a fool? Yet he will be master of all for which I toiled and used my wisdom under the sun. This also is vanity (Ec 2:18 f.).

The matter has yet a third aspect. Besides the cutting short of his permanence and the loss of control over what he has achieved, the wise man also finds that wisdom has demanded from him sacrifice, toil, exertion and work, which now, in the light of death, are shown to be meaningless. In evaluating this aspect, the attitude of hatred of life is now accompanied by disillusion.

> So I turned about and gave my heart up to despair over all the toil of my labors under the sun, because sometimes a man who has toiled with wisdom and knowledge and skill must leave all to be enjoyed by a man who did

> not toil for it. This also is vanity and a great evil. What
> has a man from all the toil and strain for which he toils
> beneath the sun? For all his days are full of pain, and
> his work is a vexation; even in the night his mind does
> not rest. This also is vanity (Ec 2:20–23).

Thus death, as the mind becomes aware of it, deprives the wisdom of the wise of its meaning in an increasingly radical way. Death has become the frontier situation which forces man to reflect upon it and leads him through this reflection toward a new attitude, that of hatred of life and disillusion. Has Qoheleth now reached his conclusion? No, this is only the first step in his thought.

We now come to the second step, which is given once again in an anticipatory summary:

> There is nothing better for a man than that he should
> eat and drink, and find enjoyment in his toil. This also,
> I saw, is from the hand of God; for apart from him who
> can eat or who can have enjoyment? (Ec 2:24.)

Thus the second step in his thinking leads to a new love for life, one based upon God. The object of this is the happiness of the present moment, which should be embraced with joy.

This second step in the argument has become necessary because the crisis in the happiness which is possible for man, which is brought about by the knowledge of death, cannot prevail against the fact that the practical happiness which man cannot have forever, but can possess at least for the present moment, is something positive. Consequently, he now concentrates his thought upon the present moment and what it brings. He asks where the value of the present moment comes from, and reaches the conclusion that God is behind everything. All human plans must fail, because death and fate frustrate them. Every moment of time has its own content, which is controlled from elsewhere. This idea is set out first of all in a great poem which appeals to experience:

> For everything there is a season,
> and a time for every matter under heaven;
>
> a time to be born, and a time to die;
> a time to plant, and a time to pluck up what is planted;

a time to kill, and a time to heal;
a time to break down, and a time to build up;
a time to weep, and a time to laugh,
a time to mourn, and a time to dance;
a time to cast away stones, and a time to gather stones
 together;
a time to embrace, and a time to refrain from embracing;
a time to seek, and a time to lose;
a time to keep, and a time to cast away;
a time to rend, and a time to sew;
a time to keep silence, and a time to speak;
a time to love, and a time to hate;
a time for war, and a time for peace (Ec 3:1–8).

The consequence drawn from this catalog based on experience is given in the form of a rhetorical question:

What gain has the worker from his toil? (Ec 3:9.)

The actual filling of the course of time with reality is not governed by human plans, but from elsewhere. If it is governed from elsewhere, then it is clear to Qoheleth, without further discussion, that it is governed by God. Thus he at once goes on to set out the true "business that God has given to the sons of men to be busy with":

He has made everything beautiful in its time; also he has extended the human consciousness over the whole course of time (R.S.V. "he has put eternity into man's mind") yet so man cannot find out what God has done from the beginning to the end (Ec 3:11).

This seems to me to be the correct interpretation of this verse, which is difficult to translate. It is not a human plan, but the beautiful plan of God which is realized in time. It is the work of God, and not of men, which is done. Man cannot comprehend the divine plan, although at the same time he has the need to be aware of it or at least to have before him a plan which fills the whole of time — for God has "put the whole course of time into the heart" (as the passage reads literally). Thus bearing in mind the ruin of all his own works by the inevitable arrival of death, and the inscrutability of the whole of the work of God in time, man is forced to limit himself to the present moment. What

is given to him in the present moment is given from God, so
that he may bring himself into accord with the word of God, even
if he cannot comprehend it. This work of God endures forever
(Ec 3:14 f.). If man subjects himself to what the present moment
brings him from God, then he is practicing religion or, in the
words of the ancient Near East, the fear of God. This gives a key
to the meaning of the next statement of Qoheleth:

> God has made it so, in order that men should fear before
> him (Ec 3:14).

Thus if at any given moment man receives happiness and joy
either because of his own wise actions or simply through God's
providence (cf. Ec 2:25 f.), he fears God, if he accepts this as a
gift of God. This is the best thing which is given to man in his
existence:

> I know that there is nothing better for them than to be
> happy and enjoy themselves as long as they live; also
> that it is God's gift to man that everyone should eat
> and drink and take pleasure in all his toil (Ec 3:12 f.).

This is the final attitude to which Qoheleth has sought to
lead man by the consideration of death: the acceptance of the gift
of happiness in the present moment from the hand of God.

What Qoheleth has worked out in coherent terms in the second and third chapters of his book, he now takes up again and
again in the more loosely arranged remaining chapters, illustrating
it first from one point of view and then from another. His statements are interspersed with traditional rules of wisdom, intended
to help a young man to make plans to find his way in the world;
Qoheleth has not completely rejected human plans, but only
shown that they are relative and meaningless when the question
of their ultimate significance is posed. This relativity is now illustrated by other human experiences, those of the injustice of the
world, the blindness of fate, and suffering.

We shall conclude by choosing from all these texts one which
once again argues closely the connection between the consideration of death and the command to accept the joy of the present
moment:

Then I saw all the work of God, that man cannot find out the work that is done under the sun. However much man may toil in seeking, he will not find it out; even though a wise man claims to know, he cannot find it out.

But all this I laid to heart, examining it all, how the righteous and the wise and their deeds are in the hand of God, whether it is love or hate man does not know . . . one fate comes to all, to the righteous and the wicked, to the good and the evil, to the clean and the unclean, to him who sacrifices and him who does not sacrifice. As is the good man, so is the sinner; and he who swears is as he who shuns an oath. This is an evil in all that is done under the sun, that one fate comes to all, also the hearts of men are full of evil, and madness is in their hearts while they live, and after that they go to the dead. But he who is joined with all the living has hope, for a living dog is better than a dead lion. For the living know that they will die, but the dead know nothing, and they have no more reward; but the memory of them is lost. Their love and their hate and their envy have already perished, and they have no more for ever any share in all that is done under the sun.

Go, eat your bread with enjoyment, and drink your wine with a merry heart; for God has already approved what you do. Let your garments be always white; let no oil be lacking on your head. Enjoy life with the wife whom you love, all the days of your vain life which he has given you under the sun, because that is your portion in life and in your toil at which you toil under the sun. Whatever your hand finds to do, do it with your might; for there is no work or thought or knowledge or wisdom in Sheol, to which you are going (Ec 8:17–9:10).

That this call to joy is seen as a religious call is shown by Ecclesiastes 12:1, a verse which itself occurs in the middle of such a call to joy:

Remember also your Creator in the days of your youth, before the evil days come, and the years draw nigh, when you will say: "I have no pleasure in them."

Qoheleth's consideration of death, which in many respects can be compared with the arguments of modern philosophers, but which knows hatred of life and disillusion only as an intermediate stage, and asserts the enjoyment of life as the conclusion, makes at one and the same time a greater and more modest claim than the systematic wisdom of Proverbs 1–9. Its claim is greater because its questions are more radical, its observations more realistic, and its answers more honest. But it is more modest, for while Qoheleth still finds a meaning for everything that happens, this meaning is known only to God, and not to man, and man is forced back upon the present moment, and must humbly accept the fullness of being and joy given by God in the present moment, without looking further to see whence it comes and whither it leads. The ancient wisdom teaching of the fixed connection between human actions and their outcome has broken down, remains true only in a very provisional sense, and always can be frustrated by the work of God which is unknown to us.

This may be accepted by a man whose every moment is filled with joy. But can the philosophy of Qoheleth satisfy someone who is undergoing misfortune, and to whom Qoheleth can only say that this too comes from God, and is followed by death? In a late period of Israel's history, a new solution was thought out, as soon as belief in the resurrection of the dead appeared.

### Death in the Thought of the Wisdom of Solomon

The Book of Wisdom deals with our problem in chapters 1–5. It begins with the call to live a just and wise life, and at once asserts, as a warning against foolishness, the fixed principle of the connection between actions and their outcome, guaranteed by the omniscience of the Spirit of God and by the judgment which is exercised upon all human action:

> For wisdom is a kindly spirit
> and will not free a blasphemer from the guilt of his words;
> because God is witness of his inmost feelings,
> and a true observer of his heart,
> and a hearer of his tongue.
> Because the Spirit of the Lord has filled the world,
> and that which holds all things together knows what is
>     said;

therefore no one who utters unrighteous things will
     escape notice;
and justice, when it punishes, will not pass him by.
For inquiry will be made into the counsels of an ungodly
     man,
and the report of his words will come to the Lord,
to convict him of his lawless deeds;
because a jealous ear hears all things,
and the sound of murmurings does not go unheard
     (Wis 1:6–10).

What is the punishment for sin and foolishness? This question
must be posed here and leads directly to the theme of "death."
The Wisdom of Solomon, which has learned from Greek ideas,
goes on at once to a comprehensive definition of death. It is
presented neither as premature death, death as a distinct domain,
nor as the biological death on which Qoheleth casts so unrelent-
ing a light; instead, an attempt is made to give it an ontological
definition:

Do not invite death by the error of your life,
nor bring on destruction by the works of your hands;
because God did not make death,
and he does not delight in the death of the living.
For he created all things that they might exist,
and the generative forces of the world are wholesome,
and there is no destructive poison in them;
the dominion of Hades is not on earth.
For righteousness is immortal (Wis 1:12–15).

God, moral good, being and immortality are all related. Since
they exist, death is pushed out to the edge of reality. It cannot
prevail, as it undoubtedly does in Qoheleth. All this sounds very
Greek and so it is. The ultimate basis for the marginal position
of death is the irreconcilability of the idea of righteousness and
that of death. But as the book proceeds, we see that Greek
thought nevertheless has provided only words and categories. The
certainty of the statement which is made depends upon the belief
which now exists in the resurrection of the dead by God. And
the text for this is to be nothing less than a paraphrase of the
Yahwist narrative of paradise and the fall — ignoring, however, the
fact that the scope of the latter does not extend to biological

death, and that "death" and "life" in it are entities existing in separate domains within this world. That it is Genesis 1–3 which the book has in mind can be seen from the next chapter, where the reference is clearer:

> For God created man for incorruption,
> and made him in the image of his own eternity,
> but through the devil's envy death entered the world,
> and those who belong to his party experience it (Wis 2:23 f.).

Thus the same situation is present as in Proverbs 1–9 and in the older proverbial wisdom. Death threatens only the wicked. There is a way of avoiding it, the way shown by wisdom. The difference is that this way is no longer understood as lying within this world, but looks beyond the limits placed by biological death. "Death" is a threatening reality (or more precisely a non-reality) lying beyond biological death.

In chapter 2 the Book of Wisdom examines more fully the close link between the godless and death. This is done in a literary fashion, by presenting the godless as making a speech in which their view is set out. This speech shows — according to the interpretative introduction which the book itself provides — that the ungodly actually "by their words and deeds summon death; considering him a friend, they find a way, and they make a covenant with him" (Wis 1:16). The speech of the ungodly evidently — especially to someone who turns to it from Qoheleth — consists of two parts. In the first part the basic ideas of Qoheleth are set out, with a certain triteness, which fails to reproduce his profound religious feeling. This does not mean that we have here a literary allusion. But it is quite evident that for the thought of this time, in which through the expectation of resurrection the link between actions and their outcome once again had become wholly fundamental, Qoheleth must have seemed to be keeping dangerous company:

> For they reasoned unsoundly, saying to themselves,
> "Short and sorrowful is our life,
> and there is no remedy when a man comes to his end,
> and no one has been known to return from Hades.

> Because we were born by mere chance
> and hereafter we shall be as though we had never been;
> because the breath in our nostrils is smoke,
> and reason is a spark kindled by the beating of our hearts.
> When it is extinguished, the body will turn to ashes,
> and the spirit will dissolve like empty air.
> Our name will be forgotten in time,
> and no one will remember our works;
> our life will pass away like the traces of a cloud,
> and be scattered like mist
> that is chased by the rays of the sun
> and overcome by its heat.
> For our allotted time is the passing of a shadow,
> and there is no return from our death,
> because it is sealed up and no one turns back.
> Come, therefore, let us enjoy the good things that exist,
> and make use of the creation to the full as in youth.
> Let us take our fill of costly wine and perfumes,
> and let no flower of spring pass by us.
> Let us crown ourselves with rosebuds before they wither.
> Let none of us fail to share in our revelry
> everywhere let us leave signs of enjoyment,
> because this is our portion, and this is our lot" (Wis 2:1–9).

At this point, however, the speech of the ungodly takes a new turn. In a few transitional verses ethical standards are shown to disappear: "But let our might be our law of right, for what is weak proves itself to be useless" (Wis 2:11). Then what they are really concealing is manifested: the hatred of the righteous man, who is a constant reproach to them:

> Let us lie in wait for the righteous man,
> because he is inconvenient to us and opposes our actions;
> he reproaches us for sins against the law,
> and accuses us of sins against our training.
> He professes to have knowledge of God,
> and calls himself a child of the Lord.
> He became to us a reproof of our thoughts;
> the very sight of him is a burden to us,
> because his manner of life is unlike that of others,
> and his ways are strange.
> We are considered by him as something base,
> and he avoids our ways as unclean;
> he calls the last end of the righteous happy,

and boasts that God is his father.
Let us see if his words are true,
and let us test what will happen at the end of his life;
for if the righteous man is God's son, he will help him,
and will deliver him from the hands of his adversaries.
Let us test him with insult and torture,
that we may find out how gentle he is,
and make trial of his forbearance.
Let us condemn him to a shameful death,
for, according to what he says, he will be protected
    (Wis 2:12–20).

This portrayal is a long way from the ancient proverbial wisdom. Now the normal fate of the righteous is premature death. This is prepared for him by sinners, who themselves enjoy happiness and life. But it is now no longer thought right to restrict one's consideration to what lies on this side of the limit laid down by biological death. And therefore in Chapter 3 the full reality is revealed:

But the souls of the righteous are in the hand of God,
and no torment will ever touch them.
In the eyes of the foolish they seemed to have died,
and their departure was thought to be an affliction,
and their going from us to be their destruction;
but they are at peace.
For though in the sight of men they were punished,
their hope is full of immortality (Wis 3:1–4).

The certain provision of happiness for the righteous man after his death is discussed in the verses that follow, with regard to two particular examples, that of the childless woman (who according to the view of ancient times had been afflicted by God) (Wis 3:13–4:2), and that of the righteous man who dies early (Wis 4:7–16).

The lot of sinners who have been happy upon earth will be different after their death:

After this day they will become dishonored corpses,
and an outrage among the dead for ever;
Because he will dash them speechless to the ground,
and shake them from the foundations;
they will be left utterly dry and barren,

and they will suffer anguish,
and the memory of them will perish.
They will come with dread when their sins are reck-
oned up,
and their lawless deeds will convict them to their face
(Wis 4:18 f.).

Then they will see the righteous man standing up confident, and
— too late — will speak to one another in remorse and acknowledge their error (Wis 5:4–13). Thus to sum up:

Because the hope of the ungodly man is like chaff
carried by the wind,
and like a light hoarfrost driven away by a storm;
it is dispersed like smoke before the wind,
and it passes like the remembrance of a guest who stays
but a day.
But the righteous live for ever
and their reward is with the Lord;
the Most High takes care of them (Wis 5:14 f.).

This brings to a conclusion the consideration of death in the
Book of Wisdom. A new theme begins in Chapter 6.

In the Book of Wisdom death is only apparently the end. In
reality it is the entry (observe the words "departure" and "going"
in 3:2 f.) into the realm of truth. What has been previously concealed is now revealed. What has previously been held back is
now vouchsafed. One leaves the realm of delusion, where those
who are false are on top, and those who are righteous underneath.
From this vision of death there is only one conclusion for man:
to follow the way of wisdom, righteousness and piety. It must
be expected that that way will be painful before death, and bring
suffering. But this will make all the more glorious the just reward
which God is holding ready after death. For the sake of this
reward it is now worth while to take on a heavy burden.

The purpose of the first six chapters of the Book of Wisdom is
to exhort and to console. They are addressed to believers who are
suffering misfortune in the midst of an unbelieving but happy
world — very often because of their faith itself. They are shown
the immortality which they have to hope for and to gain beyond
death. This is their rich reward, their comfort and their hope.

Death is the end and a terror only for the ungodly. For the believer it is the entry into reality. One can face it with courage.

### Final Considerations

Thus Old Testament man adopted very different attitudes toward death. It is hardly possible to reduce Proverbs 1–9, Qoheleth,
and Wisdom 1–6 logically to a common denominator. What does
this mean for us?

Anyone who holds the theological view that all books of the
holy scriptures are inerrant in the sense in which their original
authors meant them, will find himself faced here with insuperable
difficulties. In Book IV of his *Dialogues*, Gregory the Great posed
this problem in very acute terms, and tried to solve it for the
book of Qoheleth by defining his literary categories more precisely. Perhaps we have here the oldest attempt to deal with
problems of the inerrancy of the Bible by means of form criticism.
Gregory argues as follows:

> The book of Solomon in which these things are written
> is called Ecclesiastes. But Ecclesiastes really means a
> speaker before an assembly. And in the speech made by
> such a speaker, an opinion is put forward by which the
> dissension of the tumultuous people is assuaged. And
> when many have different views, they are led to a single
> opinion by the reasoning of the speaker. This book, then,
> is called the "Speaker before the Assembly," because in
> it Solomon as it were takes up the opinions of the noisy
> crowd, in order to utter them by way of an inquiry into
> what an inexperienced mind may think in temptation.
> For the diverse opinions he utters in his experiment are
> as many as the different views he has perceived. But like
> a true speaker before an assembly, he quiets the tumult
> which all are making by stretching out his hand, and
> brings them to a single opinion, which he utters at the
> conclusion of the same book: "Let us all hear together
> the goal of all this speaking; fear God, and keep his
> commandments; for this is the whole man." For if in
> this book he had not spoken in many persons, why did
> he admonish all together to head the end of all this
> speaking? Thus when he says at the end of the book,
> "Let us all hear together," he himself bears witness that

by speaking in many persons, he did not speak as though he were alone. Therefore there are some opinions which are put forward in this book by way of experiment, and others which are clear from reason. There are some which he puts forward as from the mind of one who is tempted, and is still giving himself to the pleasures of this world, and others in which he puts forward what is reasonable, in order to lead the soul away from sensual delight. Thus in one place he says, "This I saw to be good, that man should eat and drink and find enjoyment in his toil." And much further on he notes: "It is better to go into a house of mourning than a house of rejoicing." But if it is good to eat and drink, it would seem to be better to go into a house of rejoicing than into a house of mourning. This shows that he makes the former statement in the person of those who are weak, but adds the latter as the conclusion of reason. For immediately after it he gives the reason, and shows what is the use of a house of mourning, saying, "For in it the end of all men is known, and a man who is alive thinks of what he is to be."

"What he is to be," for Gregory naturally refers, in the sense of the Wisdom of Solomon, to life after death. Thus he succeeds in taking the edge off all statements in Qoheleth which are dangerous to belief in life beyond death, and even brings Qoheleth on to his own side. The whole of the Middle Ages read Qoheleth with his eyes. At the end of the Middle Ages we read in the Chapter of Book I of the *Imitation of Christ* of Thomas à Kempis:

Vanity of vanities, and all its vanity, but to love God and serve him alone (Ec 1:2). This is the highest wisdom, by despising the world, to make progress towards the kingdom of heaven. It is vanity, therefore, to seek perishing riches, and to trust in them. Vanity also it is, to court honors, and to lift up one's self on high. Vanity it is to follow the desires of the flesh, and to desire that for which hereafter there must be a heavy penalty. Vanity is to wish a long life, and take but little pains about a good life. Vanity is to attend only to the present life, and not to look forward to the things that are to come. It is vanity to love what is passing away with all speed, and not to be hastening thither where endless joy abideth. Oftentimes call to mind the proverb: The eye is not satisfied with seeing, nor is the ear filled with hearing (Ec 1:8). Study, therefore, to wean thy heart from the love of visible things, and to betake thee to the things unseen; for they that follow the pleasures of their senses, sully their conscience and lose the grace of God.

Nothing can be said against what is being put forward here. Thomas is expressing the thoughts of the Wisdom of Solomon in the language of the *devotio moderna*. But what is startling to us is that all this is supposed to be derived from the book of Qoheleth. Gregory really had succeeded in rendering this dangerous book harmless. It was read as a call to flee the world. It is Luther who first appears to have understood once again what Qoheleth is really saying. In any case, we can no longer follow Gregory at the present day. However interesting it may be that he is already solving problems concerning the inerrancy of the Bible with the aid of form criticism, his concrete view of the book of Qoheleth is nevertheless false. We must leave in being the tensions which exist between different representatives of the wisdom of the Old Testament, when they speak of man as he faces death. But which statement is true for us? Which of them is uttering the word of God?

For Christians, the question must be answered from the New Testament. In this case, moreover, there is no contradiction between the latter and rabbinic Judaism. Jesus and the whole New Testament held the same view as the Book of Wisdom. By the premature and unjust death of Jesus, and his resurrection and exaltation, a final authentication is given to Wisdom 1–6. Knowledge of life beyond death was thereby brought into the center of our faith. Paul writes:

Now if Christ is preached as raised from the dead, how can some of you say that there is no resurrection of the dead? But if there is no resurrection of the dead, then Christ has not been raised; if Christ has not been raised, then our preaching is in vain and your faith is in vain. We are even found to be misrepresenting God, because we testified of God that he raised Christ, whom he did not raise if it is true that the dead are not raised. For if the dead are not raised, then Christ has not been raised. If Christ has not been raised, your faith is futile, and you are still in your sins. Then those also who have fallen asleep in Christ have perished. If for this life only we have hoped in Christ we are of all men most to be pitied (1 Cor 15:12–19).

Thus it is no longer possible to go back behind the Book of Wisdom. The older views put forward by Israelite wisdom have been superseded, and by comparison with the total message of the one scripture can no longer claim to be the word of God. However legitimate it may have been at the time when Proverbs and Ecclesiastes were composed to think their thoughts and to live according to them, it is no longer possible today. Is it therefore as though these books no longer formed part of the scripture?

Here our inquiry into the validity of the scripture has reached its decisive point. Is it sufficient to assert that particular books of the Old Testament have been superseded by later books? With all caution, we shall show how far Proverbs and Ecclesiastes can still possess an enduring significance.

Our first consideration proceeds from observations which we have already made. The different texts we have studied have a dialectical relationship to one another. Even if one does not assume their literary dependence, that is, if one does not accept that each later writer had before him the previous text which we have studied, and wrote in opposition to them, yet at least each successive view always contradicts the view represented by the preceding book. But such a dialectic connection signifies that the early stage has not merely been abandoned but is at the same time preserved in a different form in the later stage. In Wisdom 1–6 the ancient doctrine of the firm connection between action and its consequences, which Qoheleth appeared to have destroyed, in fact returns. But in Wisdom 1–6, Qoheleth's insight into the worthlessness of everything in this world and the attention he pays to the fact that death affects all men, and not merely sinners, also is effective. Thus the earlier stages of Israelite thought about death perceive and describe in profound terms aspects of reality which are still valid at later stages — even if they are found in a different total context. Since the last stage can already assume that the previous stages are present in the consciousness of the reader, they need not place any great importance upon giving an account of them, and can devote most of their attention to what is new in their own statement.

Thus anyone who seeks to understand everything that the final stage has to say must read not only the document produced at this stage, but must also follow, in his consideration of death, the whole process which led to the final stage. This is necessary to a particular degree at present. The intellectual environment in which we live is at the stage of Qoheleth rather than that of the Wisdom of Solomon. One has only to think of the importance of existential philosophy for the contemporary understanding. Thus if we do not wish to accept the message of the Book of Wisdom in such a superficial sense that what we have to say is credible neither to ourselves nor to other men of our own age, we must first have experienced the crisis to which Qoheleth gives expression. The Book of Wisdom is worthy of belief only if it is accepted in faith against this background.

Here we may add a second consideration. We often hear today of the "disappearance of faith" which can be observed in our time. The faith which is "disappearing," if we consider it more closely, is often faith in the world to come. Even those who are not conscious that this is happening in their own minds reveal it in certain symptoms: the veneration of the saints is declining, few indulgences are gained for the "souls of the departed," the words "save your soul" are no longer heard. These symptoms are often explained in a positive sense: attention is now being concentrated on the central issue, it is christocentric, and so forth.

We do not wish to reject this explanation altogether. But are not the primary causes quite different? Does not the disappearance of certain traditional forms of devotion reveal in the first instance simply the influence of a modern understanding which is radically concentrated upon this world? The objective form which this understanding takes for us is a world view which, in its very structure, is wholly concerned with this world, and on which it is impossible simply to construct a world beyond this one. We all possess this view of the world, even those of us who believe. Consequently, the statements of faith concerning the world to come lose their color and their power, even though in theory — when one is asked about the matter — one naturally affirms them.

The question is this: Can anyone who accepts the doctrines of faith concerning the world to come in abstract terms, but for whom they have become meaningless and have lost their force, still be called a Christian? Is there any possibility of a belief in Christ which is experienced purely in terms of this world? Is it possible to have a loving submission to the mystery of Christ and an acceptance in hope of the atonement he has carried out, without there being a firm connection between this and the world to come, and without the principal emphasis in our faith and hope being rooted there?

We repeat, we are not dealing here with the denial of fundamental statements of the Christian gospel, but with the role which they play in the actual consciousness of the hard-pressed Christians of the present day. When we look at the Old Testament, we must acknowledge that it was possible to believe, hope and love, without a vision of the world to come. We hold the view that Abraham and the other righteous men of the Old Covenant already had faith. At the same time, we know that the vision of a world beyond was barred to them. Thus faith, hope and love in a seminal form must be possible, even if one's philosophy is like that of the Book of Proverbs or Qoheleth. Certainly, it is no longer possible at the present day for the Church, acting as a whole and teaching authoritatively, to acknowledge such a philosophy and at the same time reject in theory the philosophy of the Book of Wisdom.

The Church must always attempt to bring as many men as possible to a full and complete consciousness of the faith. But within the Church it is nevertheless possible that individual men, or perhaps even groups and generations, once again may be closer, in what determines their actual understanding, to Qoheleth than to the Wisdom of Solomon. As a Christian, therefore, one should not despair when one perceives that one can no longer make sense of the truths concerning the world to come — even though one loves Christ and commits oneself to the mystery of Christ in faith and in the hope of atonement. Such a person can be assured that he is not the first who has followed such a path, and should know the part of the Bible in which the basic images of this form of faith can be found. At the same time, the pastor who encounters such persons should not dismiss them hastily as victims of the general "disappearance of faith" who are virtually lost, but rather should proceed from an acceptance that with all the limitations of their view, they perhaps have a very lively, pure and — in many respects — heroic faith.

We should not assume from the first that by dint of proper instruction and through an effort on the part of the person concerned, everything can be brought back to normal. Neither should be absent. But it is far from certain that as individuals we can make our way against the overwhelming tendency of our world. Thus the pastor, in the end, should not be disturbed. He should simply ask whether these persons would really lack anything if, having opened their hearts in this world to the mystery of God endlessly present in Christ and his Church, they rose again and were to see that this mystery only manifests its full glory upon a new earth?

Finally, a third consideration. We regard the shift in emphasis within the understanding of faith by man as the effect upon Christians of the contemporary modern consciousness as a whole, formed as it is by unbelief. But is it possible that there may be more in it than that and that a development may be present here which can be justified in genuine Christian terms? Perhaps it was necessary that the gospel of the resurrection of the dead, which was new at the time when the old covenant was drawing to its close, should first drive into the background, in order to prevail itself, other truths and the attitudes appropriate to them?

Did the thought of the time perhaps lead to an excessive diversion of attention toward the world to come on the part of Christianity, perhaps under the influence of the note sounded by Paul in I Corinthians 15? If this is so, the moment for it to pass away has now arrived. The Church at the present day is turning anew to earthly reality. One must naturally ask whether the Church is sinning here, or is guided by the Holy Spirit. Some things which happened at the Council suggest that the latter is the case. Must such a new direction of attention toward what is present and earthly not have its consequences for the structure of the understanding of the faith? It is impossible ever to reach the point where belief in the world to come disappears altogether. But in the future this belief may tend to move from the central point which it previously occupied toward the periphery. It also may be that the type of person whom we sought to understand and for whom we tried to find a place is not someone whose Christianity has gone wrong and whose existence belongs to the margin of Christianity, but a transitional phenomenon of great importance for the future. Though he may temporarily fall into the other extreme, he may be aiding the development of a Christianity better balanced than before in its attitude to this world and the next. In this case, the groups of statements in the Old Testament which do not yet take into account the world to come would obtain a new actuality. This is only a possibility, and nothing more. Yet, we repeat once again, in these considerations we are not dealing with the truth or falsehood of de fide statements concerning the world to come, but only with the position they are accorded in the concrete Christian understanding.

CARMELITE MONASTERY
Beckley Hill
Barre, Vt., 05641

DATE BORROWED
OCT 17 1969